GLOW UP YOUR LIFE

100 MICRO HABITS
FOR
MEGA WELL-BEING

by
Victoria Contoret

N.E.O.PEOPLE

2024

LEGAL PAGE

Self-Published on Kindle and
Amazon's Print-on-Demand Service
Copyright © 2024 Victoria Contoret. All Rights Reserved.

This book is not a theoretical treatise but a practical guide to your inner world, which we call the N.E.O.Home. Management in this world is accomplished through habits and N.E.O.Pauses - practices that you will encounter in the pages of the book. All you have to do is read the instructions and do the practice without procrastination. Any practice of N.E.O.Pauses takes no more than 3 minutes and gives a tangible result of an inflow of vital energy "in the moment."

Ownership Rights Notice

This book is protected by copyright. It is intended for personal use only. You may not copy, distribute, sell, or use the entire book or any part of it for commercial purposes without the author's consent and agreement on the terms

Collaboration Notice

The author welcomes all forms of honest business collaboration to promote the content of this book, the practices described, the meditations, and the underlying philosophies. We are open to considering partnerships within existing N.E.O.Projects or creating new forms of information sharing to foster human Well-Being. Please send your proposals and suggestions to victoria@1234neo.com.

Liability Notice

The author of this book accepts responsibility for the accuracy of the information presented here, as it arises from personal life experience, beliefs, and understanding of Well-Being. The author takes responsibility for their own life and Well-Being. As a unique individual, each reader holds sole responsibility for their own life. Readers are encouraged to use their awareness and judgment before applying the author's recommendations. The author does not guarantee specific outcomes from following the habits and practices described in this book. Individual experiences may vary, and the effectiveness of these practices may depend on factors such as honesty, consistency, discipline, and the reader's personal choices within life circumstances.

This book is intended to inspire and guide readers on their personal journey to Well-Being. The recommendations provided are not therapeutic and do not replace professional advice or treatment. Always prioritize your physical, mental, and emotional health.

By using the information in this book, you acknowledge that you are responsible for your own Well-Being and that the author cannot be held liable for any consequences arising from the application of the information contained herein.

Dedication

*I dedicate this book to my mother,
who laid the foundation of my Well-Being
through family traditions, habits,
and a sense of responsibility.*

You don't need to dispel the darkness;

it is enough to radiate light!

N.E.O.PEOPLE

The way we live, how we look, how healthy we are,

self-realized, materially secure and

in harmonious relationships –

is 90% the result of our habits.

Η συνήθεια είναι δεύτερη φύση (Αριστοτέλης)

Habit is second nature. (Aristotle)

This Book Was Written Without Artificial Intelligence

WHAT IS THIS BOOK ABOUT, AND FOR WHOM IS IT?

Do you know that our reality - the event series of our lives - is 90% formed from established habits, i.e. patterns of action, behavior, thinking, and reacting that we are accustomed to? We have created our own lives to be entirely our own doing.

The good news is that we can change our reality by changing our habits.

This book is not just and not so much about formally changing habits but rather about embracing the global changes we want to bring into our lives.

Making and replacing habits brings a tangible change in life. This is Voluntary Exit from the Comfort Zone in a Given Direction (this is also the name of my author's Self-Development Methodology - author's note). Working with habits is a conscious shaping of your life. It is the creation of your reality.

Therefore, the book is for those who are open to change, want to change themselves, and want to change life around them, understanding and accepting full responsibility for this.

This book is for the conscious and aware, for every living person.

TO THE READER

Dear reader! This book fell into your hands not by chance. In this space and time, nothing is random at all. And the way I wrote this book, and the way I talked to each of the readers, and to you too - all this is not by chance either.

The 100 Habits of Well-Being are important and useful for everyone who has taken responsibility for their life and, therefore, is on the direct path to their Well-Being.

Everyone's Well-Being is different. It is impossible to describe it, to put it into some standards frameworks, or to offer a template for receiving benefits. It is impossible because every person on the planet is unique.

We have unique fingerprints, retinas, and the construction of energy fields and interactions, which we call the N.E.O.Home in our project. Every N.E.O.HuMan - a HuMan with New Awareness, ECO-Mind and Open Heart should have their own home.

For the N.E.O.HuMan, this is their N.E.O.Home - their bright, clean, prosperous inner space, which is reflected in the event series of everyday life for each of us. The cleaner, more balanced, calmer and more benevolent we are inside, the more prosperous our life.

For me, Well-Being is a state of inner pleasure and satisfaction. Some people need to have a lot of friends for this state, and for some people, one faithful friend is enough. For some people, the balance of inner Well-Being depends on noisy actions and joyful parties, and for some people, solitude, contemplation, and reflection with a good book are valuable.

Some people need to have luxurious material support for Well-Being, and some live in reasonable sufficiency. There is no mistake here - each variant is correct and unique, that is why it is impossible to formulate the concept of Well-Being other than the inner state of harmony and joy in the heart.

In order for this book to be successful in your hands and in your life, answer yourself the main question: Have you already made a choice about your life? Have you chosen a Life of Joy and Well-Being? If so, then from today on, beautiful transformations will begin to take place in your life.

As you read this book and work with the N.E.O.Workbook we have created specifically to help you, you will see your life aligning into prosperous events, circumstances, and relationships. New doors will open to you, behind which new opportunities await you, and only you will have to decide whether you will enter this or that door.

Before you take a step forward, ask yourself: "Does this step lead to my Well-Being, my inner harmony, my satisfaction with myself and my life?" If yes, then step boldly towards the changes. Accept them with an open heart and give the world light and smiles, your creativity and your work. Take care of other people and yourself. Live a Prosperous Life.

TABLE OF CONTENTS

Legal page 2
What is this book about, and for whom is it? 5
To the reader 6
Glossary 11
When, where, and why was this book born? 14
Chapter 1. We all want Well-Being 17

What is a habit? 17
Where are habits stored? 17
Why do we need habits, and how can we apply them to live in the flow? 18
Methodology for developing habits 20
Real benefits of consciously developed habits 21
The result of a habit is not immediately visible, consider cumulative effects 22
What is Well-Being 24

Chapter 2. The foundation of Well-Being – the N.E.O.HOME 27

Everyone has their Own N.E.O.HOME 27
We attract what we are attuned to 27
We must take care of our Well-Being 28

Chapter 3. Habits of Well-Being and the formation of reality – your smart N.E.O.HOME 30

Smart N.E.O.HOME – managing your inner space 30
Conscious management of your inner space is the foundation of the Well-Being of our life 31
So what is the smart N.E.O.HOME technology? 33
What can we control with the smart N.E.O.HOME technology? 35
What is the technology itself? 35
Regular training is the key to success 37
Activate your smart N.E.O.HOME to develop new habits of Well-Being 38

Chapter 4. Paths to Well-Being 41

What kinds of benefits are there 41

The mind and the heart. Balance 43
"Mine - Not Mine" Test 47
Gratitude is a tool of cosmic scale 51
Purity of intentions on the path to Well-Being is the key 55
Trust and ease 55
Simple signs of a trusting life path 57
What can you wish for? 58
Spiritual maturity of desires 60

Chapter 5. 12 foundations of Well-Being — how to create your abundant reality 62

1st, self-care is taking care of your mental balance 63
Care no. 2 is taking care of your spine 64
Care no. 3 is taking care of body flexibility 64
4th care is taking care of the skin and hair 65
5th care is taking care of relationships 65
6th care is taking care of the purity of your vibrations 66
Care no. 7, and here we are talking about purity in its usual sense 67
Care no. 8 is taking care of joy and ease 67
Care no. 9 is taking care of meanings 67
10th care is taking care of moving forward 68
Care no. 11 is taking care of beauty and pleasantness for the five senses 69
Care no. 12 is taking care of financial and material sufficiency 69

Chapter 6. Three live N.E.O.SKILLS of Well-Being 72

The first skill is a good mood. 73
The second skill is healthy eating. 74
The third skill is the skill of self-care. 75
How does life change with live skills? 76

Chapter 7. Catalog of 100 micro habits for mega Well-Being 78

1st sphere. Mood 78
2nd sphere. Thoughts 81
3rd sphere. Speech 83
4th sphere. Body 85

5th sphere. Food 88
6th sphere. Relationships 90
7th sphere. Housekeeping (everyday life) 92
8th sphere. Travel 95
9th sphere. Rhythm 97
10th sphere. Money 100

Chapter 8. Voluntary exit from the comfort zone in a given direction 103

Changing habits is possible, easy, and pleasant. 103
How to understand the usefulness or harmfulness of certain habits for yourself? 105
Habit as an assistant in neutralizing stress and tension 108
Discipline is different: volitional and natural 109
Helpful tips for new habits 110
What is more important in developing a habit – meaning or methodology? 111
Taking inventory of your habits is a useful thing. 112
Frequency and purity of habits 113
What helps in developing a new habit? 115
What to do if there is resistance to a new habit? 116
How many habits does a person need for a prosperous life? 118

Chapter 9. Daily Well-Being rituals 119

You need to take care of your Well-Being 119
The more we thank, the more life energy comes to us 120
Practices of a resourceful state 123
Morning rituals for a prosperous day 124
Evening rituals for good sleep and a prosperous tomorrow 129
Micro rituals - N.E.O.pauses for maintaining a prosperous day 130
Joy is the state of the new time 132
The practice of admiration 133
Raising vibrations with sound 134
How to maintain a resourceful state throughout the day 135

Conclusion and wishes 138
Gratitude 140

GLOSSARY

The book uses some terms, and the correct understanding of them will ensure the correct perception of the conveyed meanings.

Well-Being is a complex holistic state of a person, his peacefulness, confidence in himself and tomorrow, and balanced harmony, which is manifested by calm, quiet joy in the soul without conditions and reasons.

Affirmation - a positive statement, a brief phrase of self-attunement, creating a stable psychological position.

Meditations are various practices that make the mind clearer, help one understand oneself, and help one manage one's attention. Meditation increases awareness, reduces stress levels, promotes emotional wellness, and improves sleep and overall quality of life.

N.E.O.HuMan - A human of a new formation, living in trust in Life, in priority with Self, in service to the Whole.

The concept of N.E.O. includes:

N. - New Awareness.

Acceptance: I accept and respect human uniqueness - my own and each person's.

E. - ECO-Mind.

Love: I love what I do and do what I love.

O. - Open Heart.

Transmission: I share my joy and pass on my experiences to others.

N.E.O.Home is a person's inner space that is reflected and manifested in the event series of their daily life.

The Pyramid of Human Uniqueness by Contoret© is an indicator of a person's spiritual maturity.

According to the Pyramid of Human Uniqueness©, there are 12 Stages (levels) of human awareness. A Stage is determined by reflecting external signs of his behavior, habits, attachments and priorities (4 x P).

A 27-item questionnaire (Quantum Projector) describing a person's natural daily life determines the Stage of Awareness.

The Awareness Stage does not make us "champions" or "losers" but speaks to our spiritual maturity. Every person, regardless of their Stage of Awareness, is worthy of the love and respect of others.

N.E.O.Pause - micro-meditation, a short meditative practice lasting 1-5 minutes. It can be aimed at relaxation, finding inner balance, and mobilizing the body and concentration. It is presented in various forms, depending on the central action: breathing, silence, contemplation, chanting, and more.

An N.E.O.Practice is a brief exercise (1-5 minutes) focused on your attention and breathing, intended to bring life energy into the present moment. In this project, it is also referred to as an N.E.O.Pause.

The N.E.O.People Project is a set of author's methods, practices, meditations, courses, retreats, ways and methods of increasing a person's awareness in everyday life, aimed at acquiring Well-Being and staying in a resourceful state regardless of external circumstances.

Habit is a way of action, behavior, thinking, and reaction, brought to automatism, conditioned by current or previously acquired experience.

WHEN, WHERE, AND WHY WAS THIS BOOK BORN?

This book came to me as an epiphany. Rather, not a book came to me because its contents and the 100 Habits of Well-Being are my habits, resulting in my life being prosperous and joyful.

It wasn't always that way. Some periods of turbulence and trials in my life are a separate story, but all these habits helped me pass these trials and get out of the corkscrew fall.

My habits have always supported me by carefully and carefully preserving my life energy so that I could meet the urgent and pressing tasks and challenges that life's journey has put in front of me. Some of these habits I absorbed from my parents' house, my grandparents, and people close to me, i.e., many of them come from my childhood. But no less than half of them are already a collection of conscious age of the last 35 years of my spiritual transformation and conscious choice to create a prosperous life.

The idea of writing this book really came "in the moment." It was in 2023 in the Seychelles. I always winter there. One day, walking along the shore, I was admiring the colorful sea pebbles and their harmonious forms, and suddenly the idea arose to collect, like pebbles on the sand, 100 Habits of Well-Being from my life - all together, with the belief that this collection will bring Well-Being and joy to other people.

Another reason this bright idea visited me is that I have two grandchildren, Shanti and Samuel. Their lifestyle, of course, is quite different from their grandmother's. But as I watched the children, I realized that I have no better chance to impart all the wisdom I have gathered to them in a better form than to write a book and gift it to them with love. So, in the acknowledgments section of this book, I express my heartfelt gratitude to my grandchildren for being able to pass on my accumulated experience to them. They will most likely read this book in electronic format because they spend much time on their gadgets.

This book is for those who spend a lot of time looking at their device screen.

I have no doubt, my dear reader, that you spend a lot of time on your devices. This is normal for today's realities, so this book is designed to help you create Well-Being in your life. Rather, it will create itself, and these simple habits will help you.

It is not necessary that you will fit or like all 100, but I sincerely recommend that you try even those you do not like, and if it does not go at all, you certainly do not need to force yourself. But the magic of habits is that they save energy, which you, sitting and looking at the screen of your device, need a lot of because every gadget takes energy, but the Habits of Well-Being will help you restore vital energy, simply and without strain.

For your convenience, we have created the N.E.O.Workbook.

It will guide you toward realizing which of the habits will be useful to you and which may be objectively necessary.

I wish you success on your creative path.

With love, *Victoria Contoret*
e-mail: victoria@1234neo.com

CHAPTER 1.
WE ALL WANT WELL-BEING

WHAT IS A HABIT?

A habit is a way of acting, behaving, thinking, or reacting that has been brought to automaticity. We are not aware of all our habits, and as we already know, 90% of actions are performed by the average person in habitual, patterned ways, so we can say that we spend 90% of our lives in habits. That is why it is important that these habits do not destroy us but rather harmonize with us. They should not create resistance to the flow of life but help us fit into it beautifully.

A habit is like rails for a train. We choose the direction in which the train will go, and habits make the movement of this train smooth and pleasant so that we can sit, sip tea, and watch the changing pictures outside the window. In other words, a habit is something that does not spend the resource of our attention, i.e., our life energy, which means that a habit is a tool for regulating and preserving our life energy for living in the present moment, in the flow, in a state of balance, joy, health, and Well-Being.

WHERE ARE HABITS STORED?

Our habits are stored in the subconscious mind and are directly related to the neural network. Simply put, our habits live in our N.E.O.Home, influencing all our inner space's fields, systems, and structures. In this N.E.O.Home of ours, we can cultivate new habits, get rid of old, unnecessary, or even harmful ones, or replace some habits with others. We will discuss this in more detail below.

WHY DO WE NEED HABITS, AND HOW CAN WE APPLY THEM TO LIVE IN THE FLOW?

It may seem that habit, as a mechanical, automatic, repetitive action, contradicts the very essence of modern life - living in the flow. In fact, this is not the case. The truth is found at the point from which it can be seen that everything that makes up our life directly depends on the amount of our energy. Living in the flow, rapid changes, transformation, and ease of accepting change require a large amount of energy.

Imagine a rocket. The rocket module itself is much smaller than the rocket booster that puts the rocket module into orbit. To start, to move, to accelerate, a large amount of energy is needed, and the example of the rocket module is excellent proof of this.

Now, let's get back to balance. There is a certain set of habitual actions that we do not need to bring to the level of awareness specifically, that is, to constantly monitor which hand to insert the key into the keyhole and lock the door, how to properly brush our teeth, on which shelf to find pajamas for sleeping, in what sequence to conduct morning rituals so that the rhythm of the day does not fall apart and is harmonious - for all this we have mechanical patterns of action, and they help us save energy. This amount of saved energy will be used to live in the flow, where circumstances and situations suddenly arise that need to be reacted to promptly, positively, and rationally.

Our habits, from the point of view of life energy, are excellent helpers in keeping our energy in a resourceful state for moving through life.

Of course, some habits take away energy. We call them bad habits, and I suggest getting rid of them and replacing them with good habits.

The necessity of habits in our life is obvious. We transfer the responsibility for the expenditure of energy from the main volume of energy that we are given for each day to the level of the subconscious, and the subconscious acts according to its algorithms, thereby allowing us to easily and, without resistance, perform certain actions that are useful for us, necessary for a person's prosperous life in society.

We can compare the work of the conscious and subconscious minds to piloting an airplane. If our consciousness is the pilot, then the autopilot is our subconscious, and now, imagine: the pilot controls the plane in live mode, i.e., lives in the flow. It is not for nothing that pilots are paid a high salary, and the requirements for their physical, mental, and psychological condition are very high. The pilot's attentiveness and ability to react to rapidly changing external circumstances are key parameters for the safety of all passengers.

Pilots retire earlier because of their energy system, and with it, their attentiveness and mental and emotional stability wear out due to the constant holding of their attention at a high point of concentration.

The autopilot helps the pilot to rest and gives him the opportunity to shift his attention to something else: to eat, to be distracted, to do physically restorative exercises, breathing practices, and a lot of other things.

We can and should apply this in our lives as well, which is why N.E.O.Pauses - short practices for restoring a person's energy to a point of resourcefulness - are so popular in our N.E.O.People project.

The autopilot, in a wonderful combination with the live pilot, provides the possibility of flying long distances in difficult conditions. In the same way, our habits - in combination with conscious actions - give us the opportunity to reasonably invest our life energy in the rhythm of everyday life.

METHODOLOGY FOR DEVELOPING HABITS

There are many different methodologies, but they were all useful in the last century, just like step-by-step instructions. But now, in the new planetary energies and in the realization that each of us is unique, offering you a rigid, precise methodology for developing a habit seems to me not only unwise but also harmful. Why? It is because changes need to be felt with the heart, and developing a new habit is a change in itself, and the beginning of life changes will always come as a result of mastering a new habit.

For example, the habit of buying only on sale leads to financial scarcity. The mind, accustomed to constantly seeking cheaper and more profitable options without relying on the soul's desire to choose the most beautiful and pleasant, immediately limits the overall flow of money and affects the material and financial state of affairs.

If you have such a habit, replace it. Don't buy only what is profitable, but what is really needed or desired. Don't succumb to mass hysteria and advertising campaigns. There is no need to buy three pairs of sneakers just because they are currently at the maximum discount. Buy only one pair, but the one you like - even if there is no discount. You will be surprised but will spend much less money and not have piles in your wardrobe.

Therefore, for developing new habits, I recommend a simple methodology - listen to yourself, listen with your heart, and separate external attacks on your brain from your real desires and needs.

REAL BENEFITS OF CONSCIOUSLY DEVELOPED HABITS

Motivation from developed habits is a mechanism that helps to go through the period of habit formation easily and with pleasure.

Developing a habit always has four real benefits:

1. Habit frees up energy for living in the flow in the present moment.
2. Habit forms natural discipline, which is the basis of a prosperous life.
3. Beneficial habits increase Well-Being and improve the quality of life in four basic areas: health, relationships, self-realization, and material Well-Being.
4. Developing habits and working with them create the ability to notice other people's habits and thus better understand a person.

THE RESULT OF A HABIT IS NOT IMMEDIATELY VISIBLE, CONSIDER CUMULATIVE EFFECTS

When introducing a new habit, we must remember that in our dual reality, everything is stretched out in time. This sometimes prolongs the process and sometimes makes life easier almost immediately. Both of these effects are inherent in habits.

When we develop a habit, we may not see any result from one habit or another. From some others - an indirect and insignificant one. Only some habits have immediate results.

For example, the habit of drinking warm water in the morning *(Habit №4 "Three Waters in the Morning" from the 4th sphere: "Body")* has an almost immediate effect of improving intestinal function.

But what about those habits where the result is not immediately visible?

An example can be the habit of making the bed *(Habit №1 from the 7th sphere "Housekeeping")*. By training ourselves to make the bed, changes in life come deep and gradually because by making the bed, we simultaneously align the energy field and harmonize thoughts in our head, doing this practice consciously.

Therefore, the result is visible in the long term. According to observations from my life, among those who have the habit of making the bed and keeping it in order, I do not know anyone who would be destitute, impoverished, living in a chaotic misunderstanding of their place in this life and joy from it.

Or here's another habit of being grateful for everything *(Habit №3 from the 3rd sphere "Speech")* definitely does not give a result at the moment, but life experience shows that this habit is the main foundation for a prosperous and happy life.

Therefore, always have patience. It is generally very useful in life, and in developing a habit, it will come in handy for you.

Developing a habit is comparable to growing a flower. You know that flowers come in different varieties - annual, perennial, indoor, or garden; there are wildflowers, there are those that live on the seashore, those that grow in the desert, while others cannot live without water at all and grow in the tropics. The same goes for habits. They all take root very differently. Each has its own period of cultivation and, accordingly, the fruits - the results come at different times, in different quantities, and in different forms.

Do not forget that in our book, there are 100 habits for a reason because I do not believe that two, three, or even ten habits can create a reliable foundation for Well-Being. Choose the ones that appeal to you from these hundred habits, and most importantly, note for yourself the ones you already have and rejoice in them.

When a habit sprouts with a useful result, you may notice it, or you may not. But one thing is certain: a good habit of Well-Being - any from our catalog of 100 habits - is like a pebble in the foundation of your prosperous life.

WHAT IS WELL-BEING

Well-Being is a state that is made up of many moments that balance this state. There is the concept of social, material, mental, psychological, and emotional Well-Being. There seem to be different kinds of Well-Being, but in my opinion, this is a marketing trick.

Human Well-Being is a complex holistic state of a person's tranquility, self-confidence, and confidence in tomorrow, balanced harmony manifested by calm, quiet joy in the soul without conditions and reasons. A person who is thriving can always be seen by their eyes, the way they move and speak, and their manner of communication.

This book is about holistic Well-Being, not its segmented elements. If a person is prosperous in the material and career sphere, but their personal life, self-realization, and inner peace are in complete disarray, then such a person cannot be called thriving.

In fairness, one should note that the concept of Well-Being in the twenty-first century has changed significantly compared to the twentieth. The attitude towards life has changed, priorities have shifted, and the principles and life itself have changed in many ways.

A prosperous person of the twentieth century built their Well-Being in different energy-informational conditions than those of today. Now, the conditions are different, but the essence of the state of Well-Being at its core has remained the same - it is a harmonious balance between the spiritual and material components, the indicator of which is a feeling of inner peace and quiet joy, satisfaction, and sufficiency.

If we analyze what this point of Well-Being consists of in the twenty-first century, it turns out that the focus has largely been transferred to internal processes, whereas in the twentieth century, we were mainly guided by external ones.

Today, freedom of choice, freedom of movement, and freedom of self-expression - are the key pillars of inner balance and therefore, of Well-Being.

Life itself has shifted the focus of our attention to internal processes, which is why the N.E.O.Home has emerged in our

N.E.O.People project as the totality of all these processes, states, and reactions of a person.

CHAPTER 2.
THE FOUNDATION OF WELL-BEING – THE N.E.O.HOME

EVERYONE HAS THEIR OWN N.E.O.HOME

Each of us lives in our own reality - and our personal N.E.O.Home determines this reality. **Our habits reside in our N.E.O.Home** and have a direct impact on its state.

To gain a deeper understanding of how habits work and help us, we will examine in detail the concept of the N.E.O.Home, its functionality, and ways to make life easier by utilizing all the capabilities of our inner space.

The N.E.O.Home is a holistic homeostatic system that functions like an organism, a totality of informational field structures, their interactions, states, as well as external event series - and all this manifests in a beautiful pattern in our daily life. We influence all these at every moment with our thoughts, decisions, choices, and habits.

WE ATTRACT WHAT WE ARE ATTUNED TO

We should note that the line of external event series is formed precisely from a person's internal states, which can correspond to low vibrations (pain, fear, resentment, sadness) or have high-frequency characteristics (joy, gratitude, love). And a person, like a magnetic coil, vibrating at a certain frequency, attracts into their life events of the frequency series at which they are at a particular moment.

That is why it is so important to choose Light, to make decisions from the Light origin so that the integrity and purity of the N.E.O.Home structure are constantly maintained in its reference quality. After all, wherever we go, whatever we do, we, like a snail, carry our N.E.O.Home with us. It is very important that in our daily reality, this structure remains whole and harmonious - this is what is called a prosperous life - when we live in an easy rhythm of creating/receiving goods according to our reasonable sufficiency. That is, we are Thriving .

WE MUST TAKE CARE OF OUR WELL-BEING

When we say, "I must take care of my Well-Being, the integrity and Well-Being of my N.E.O.Home," where can we start?

I tried to approach this question from different angles, and the only working door I found is **to be yourself and resourceful**.

When we are resourceful, it means that we have a sufficient volume of energy for conscious living. In many ways, the state of "being resourceful" is determined precisely by the set of daily habits that help conserve energy and shape the relief of our lives.

A conscious person can, in detail, attentively and without tension, take care of their N.E.O.Home in all its manifestations: both the internal - peace and balance, and the external - cleanliness and coziness; and the fact that our N.E.O.Home, radiating an individual frequency of vibrations, immediately structures the reality around us, attracts certain people and events, aligns relationships, or conversely, triggers turbulence.

It is our N.E.O.Home, which cannot be designated by a lesser characteristic than a home for each spiritual entity in this Universe; it is our N.E.O.Home that is the basis, the foundation.

In order to rely on this foundation, it is necessary to be collected and attentive, so the simplest practices are training one's attentiveness. This includes harmonization of the hemispheres, various techniques that help us increase concentration, methods of working with the centers of the head and around the head, and different light practices. But it is important to be collected - this state is also formed through habits.

Regular application of various practices - both simple daily and deeper - helps enter a state of conscious living and managing one's reality over time. The basis for this is the Well-Being of our unique N.E.O.Home - this is what we need the Habits of Well-Being for.

CHAPTER 3.
HABITS OF WELL-BEING AND THE FORMATION OF REALITY – YOUR SMART N.E.O.HOME

SMART N.E.O.HOME – MANAGING YOUR INNER SPACE

It's probably no secret to anyone that our external reality is controlled from within. However, the conditions for entering this reality are such that we are not given instructions for internal management. We come into this life, and no one has told us how to manage it. We don't know how to influence our health, current events, or destiny. We don't understand how to correlate the processes inside us with what manifests outside. Often, we even think that it is not connected in any way. In fact, everything is interconnected with everything, and we can manage this.

But we are not setting the task of figuring out the global issues of management right now; we will break this topic down into elementary components, and one of these elementary components is creating your prosperous reality through the management of your inner space, which in our project we call the N.E.O.Home. Although to be precise, we call everything the N.E.O.Home: both the inner space - systems, algorithms, and their interactions; external event series, which line up in proportion to internal algorithms. We call the management of this inner space the Smart **N.E.O.Home**.

CONSCIOUS MANAGEMENT OF YOUR INNER SPACE IS THE FOUNDATION OF THE WELL-BEING OF OUR LIFE

Imagine a modern Smart Home that knows how to communicate with its owner, responding to voice (or other) commands. It's enough to say "Light" or snap your fingers - and the light turns on.

Our inner space is ready to communicate with us according to the same principle. Our inner N.E.O.Home, according to its algorithm, is initially prepared to be controlled. But it is impossible to connect the Smart N.E.O.Home system without systemic order, without a state of balance and tranquility. This state is the result of introducing certain Well-Being habits into life that form it.

Management occurs from a special vibrational attunement - the state we get into with the help of the N.E.O.Pause - a short meditative practice.

Please relax. Now is N.E.O.Pause

Right now, I suggest doing

the N.E.O.Pause "Light Point."

By doing so, we will bring ourselves into the necessary vibrational state.

First, read the instructions and then do it.

Time investment - 90 seconds

The first thing to do is to relax. The relaxation stage is very important.

We take a comfortable body position, straighten our back, open our shoulders, smile, and close our eyes. We shift our attention to the breath. We observe our breathing. We express a pure intention about what we are doing now, this N.E.O.Pause, in which we attune with the universe. We align with this day, with the current moment.

We give a clear command - with love, without tension: "I set a light point in my spiritual heart in the middle of my chest and allow myself to shine."

We hold attention at this point. We consciously return attention every time it "runs away" and again immerse it in the point. We attend to our breathing. If there are any external sounds, we attend to them as well. We do not get drawn into anything: attentive breathing and seeing your point in the center of the chest.

We say: "I allow myself to shine. I allow myself to shine. I allow myself to shine. I am shining. I am a star. I illuminate the space for myself, my loved ones, and humanity. I thank the Creator, nature, life, this day, and everything around me for this."

I will smile and open my eyes.

If you managed to get into the N.E.O.Pause, you will now feel a change in state. Your state has become calmer and more balanced. If there was tension, it is now gone. If there was fuss - there is no trace of it left. This means that you have entered the N.E.O.Pause.

What is this state? It comes with training. Regular repetition of N.E.O.Pauses helps to train this very state in yourself, from which we can control our inner space in real-time.

The technology we are talking about has at its core a clear structure of how to get into this N.E.O.Pause. Not just to sit for two or five minutes with your eyes closed but to actually enter the necessary state.

The altered state of consciousness that we enter with the help of the N.E.O.Pause is the key to the smart N.E.O.Home. It is from this altered state of consciousness that we can easily manage internal processes and, accordingly, external ones as well.

SO WHAT IS THE SMART N.E.O.HOME TECHNOLOGY?

Smart N.E.O.Home is a technology for controlling (with the help of thought or voice) the systems of our inner space through its activation.

With the help of this technology, we can control fields, organs, processes, algorithms, their interactions, and configurations - absolutely everything.

Suppose it seems to you that this statement is from the realm of fantasy. In that case, I dare to assure you that I have been successfully living in this fantasy for more than thirty years and have absolutely wonderful experiential results, so now, when in this year 2024, we are undergoing a complete restructuring of all planetary energies, these technologies are already available to us for practically everyday use.

Yes, in the year 2000, it seemed completely unrealistic. Our team has made many efforts to test and improve the method - how to activate the space inside yourself. If 20 years ago, not everything worked out for everyone, and now, at the moment of the quantum transition, the time has come when this technology has begun to work unquestionably and everywhere, then we can say it's simply because its time has really come.

That is why, this year, the N.E.O.Pause is a key tool all over the planet, and it is from it that the process of working with the Smart N.E.O.Home technology begins.

WHAT CAN WE CONTROL WITH THE SMART N.E.O.HOME TECHNOLOGY?

You can talk to all the organs, you can sort out your blood pressure, you can negotiate with any gland that is malfunctioning, not to mention such trifles as relieving a headache - this, as they say, is as easy as it gets. The most advanced is when we begin to control the event series and the external space of our lives.

What our home looks like, what kind of relationships we have, how abundance is manifested in our life, what events occur, all of this is influenced by the Smart N.E.O.Home technology.

WHAT IS THE TECHNOLOGY ITSELF?

The technology consists of the fact that from a certain state of consciousness, observing a certain technique (the one we used in the N.E.O.Pause above), we give commands to which our inner space reacts absolutely naturally.

This technique consists of three steps:

1. The first step: we express pure intention;
2. The second step: we repeat the command three times aloud or to ourselves;
3. The third and final step: we confirm the successful execution.

Example:

I express a pure intention to activate a light point in the center of my chest - this is the first step.

Second step - I activate the light point in the center of the chest, the light point in the center of the chest, and the light point in the center of the chest - we say it three times.

The third step is confirmation: the light point in the center of the chest is activated.

You need nothing special in this practice - just your attention, calmness, desire, and faith. The meaning of the practice lies in the fact that having entered an altered state of consciousness with the help of the N.E.O.Pause, we are fully concentrated inside ourselves and able to control space.

It is important to understand two things:

- **the entire system, ready to be controlled, is already waiting for us;**
- **now is the time to activate the control.**

Is this technique something new and unique? There is nothing new here - anything new is well-forgotten old, just in a different configuration, with new names - now it is called the N.E.O.Pause.

Where could we have encountered this before? In fairy tales. For example, the tale of the genies. You need to give the genie a clear command - and he will immediately execute it. But not every command, only the one that is pronounced correctly. You need to know a special spell, an algorithm. This is the very entrance inside yourself through the N.E.O.Pause.

It is necessary to enter an altered state and manifest the Smart N.E.O.Home through the three-step technique from this state. The first step is pure intention; the second step is a threefold repetition of the command, and the third step is confirmation of the successful execution of the command.

REGULAR TRAINING IS THE KEY TO SUCCESS

While performing the practices, you may feel something or not feel anything - this is normal. It is important to try and observe the result. Try and observe, and if your brain tells you: "What does the N.E.O.Pause have to do with it, the situation resolved itself," - don't fall for it. These are the tricks of the mind, which needs to rationalize everything. But you are a soul, you are an energetic entity in a protein body. So you, as a light entity, observe how it then interfaces with your reality.

The N.E.O.Pause "Light Point" is a basic practice. It is the easiest to get into. But as with any practice, training is needed. Normally, it may not work the first time; the key to success is regular training:

We set a light point, a pure intention, proclaim three times, and confirm the result.

We repeat several N.E.O.Pauses a day, and at some point, we notice that reality harmonizes in some magical way: all the surges become velvety, everything stops conditioning you, and everything kind of resolves itself. Over time, we learn to maintain such an inner state, from which we easily and with love control the outer space. Without any tension, without resistance.

Remember: You don't need to dispel the darkness; it is enough to radiate light!

And it is for this light space that the Smart N.E.O.Home technology works.

ACTIVATE YOUR SMART N.E.O.HOME TO DEVELOP NEW HABITS OF WELL-BEING

With the help of N.E.O.Pauses, all systems and processes automatically align and begin to work on autopilot.

Imagine that you enter a house with a Smart Home system, and with just one gesture, all the functions turn on: the coffee maker, the light, soft music, the lighting in the aquarium, the floor heating in the bathroom, everything turns on. The same is true in your inner system.

The only question is whether you use it or not. I suggest you use it because the Smart N.E.O.Home system is very easy to operate. Give it attention, give it faith, give it a chance. It is ready to be activated and adjust all internal processes independently, on autopilot, it is enough to do N.E.O.Pauses.

I will give you an example to clarify the difference between when we use the Smart N.E.O.Home and when we don't use this system.

Suppose you have a wooden house in the forest, and it doesn't have a Smart Home system. When you go there, you first need to chop wood, then light a stove and heat water on this stove. You heat the water, and you need to make tea. You drank tea, you need to heat water again to wash the dishes. And if you are going to do laundry, you need to bring water from the well to heat it. When you are doing all this everyday stuff, it takes a huge amount of resources. No time or energy is left to engage in self-development, a healthy lifestyle, creativity, developing your talents, or maintaining a state of joy throughout the day.

What was the Smart N.E.O.Home created for? It was created to unload from the "household chores." All these washing machines, dishwashers, and multicookers make our life easier, free up our energy, that is, our attention.

The same is true with the inner space. If you devote just a few N.E.O.Pauses a day to this and leave opportunities for the autopilot to work - self-activation, self-regulation, self-adjustment, self-healing - you no longer have to deal with it.

You don't waste time going to doctors or sorting out critical situations. Everything aligns itself for you. Your energy remains for you so you can engage in self-development, uncovering your talents, yourself, and joyful and pleasant things. You must agree that this is practical and rational. And for this, you have a tool - a practice that helps you live.

Each of you is waiting for your extraordinarily smart N.E.O.Home, and only you can be the activator. Only you know how to create comfort and warmth in your N.E.O.Home through the activation of internal systems, spaces, and algorithms, which is also facilitated by introducing 100 Habits of Well-Being into your life.

CHAPTER 4.
PATHS TO WELL-BEING

Well-Being is, in fact, one of the key concepts underlying the creative creation of the N.E.O.Home. But the concept of Well-Being has been greatly distorted and replaced; there has been a substitution of meanings, and we should understand what Well-Being really is, what meanings we put into the word, how each of us understands Well-Being for ourselves, how we relate to it and what are the ways and means of receiving benefits.

What kind of Well-Being do we want to achieve by developing beneficial habits for ourselves? We will also consider what kinds of benefits there are in general and to what extent these benefits that we want to receive from life are ours.

When I talk about the paths of benefit-receiving, perhaps someone will think we will talk about how to earn a million. But no, we will look at the issues of receiving benefits and the paths to it through the prism of the quantum reality in which we live, and you will see that everything can be much simpler and shorter than the linear perception of receiving benefits.

WHAT KINDS OF BENEFITS ARE THERE

Let's define what kinds of benefits there are so as not to fall into the stereotype of the generally accepted understanding of Well-Being and imply only some material benefits.

In reality, there are **material** and **non-material** benefits.

Material benefits include all objects of the physical world that we can touch and use - everything we need in life. Material benefits can have dynamic development - improve, be perfected.

Non-material benefits can include, for example, joy in the heart - everything that cannot be bought for money is not related to matter but is vital for us.

How else can we divide benefits into categories?

In my opinion, there are **short-term**, **long-term**, and **timeless** benefits.

Any purchase, whether it's groceries, something from things, or even a house, is an example of a short-term material benefit. A short-term non-material benefit is when, for example, we come to a parking lot, everything is full everywhere, and suddenly, a space frees up right in front of us, and we easily park. And at this point, it is a benefit for us and no less important than a material benefit.

Long-term non-material benefits are when all sorts of lucky moments, such as with parking, happen not once but constantly. The synchronicity of the space in which you live, in which your N.E.O.Home moves, is so aligned with you that everything in your life always works out easily: you need to park - voila, a space has freed up; you need to get somewhere - voila, the transport has arrived; you need to do something - the next day information about it came, an easy path has formed.

These are long-term non-material benefits - when the synchronicity of space is on our side. As for long-term material benefits, we can attribute perhaps only the purchase of a plot in a cemetery for ourselves, and if a person is tightly stuck in this Matrix, in which we, in our turn of civilization, have rolled to complete absurdity, then you can buy a really big plot - for yourself, and your husband, and your children. Such are the benefits that the Matrix can offer us.

We need to consider what benefits are offered and whether we need them.

What are timeless benefits? I thought about some examples of a material timeless benefit and couldn't think of one; I didn't find one. But when I thought about non-material timeless benefits, several examples immediately came to mind: ancestral happiness, light karma, and kind and warm relationships lasting many lives. These are the kinds of timeless benefits that exist.

THE MIND AND THE HEART. BALANCE

We live in the Matrix, and at this point, where our civilization has brought us, we are constantly influenced by the external information space, which mainly offers us material benefits that are tempting, in beautiful packages, and everything seems very logical.

Why is it logical? It is because, as a rule, the mind leads us to material benefits. When we talk about non-material benefits, the guide to them is the heart. But the heart can also lead to material benefits. Therefore, we can say that two guides lead us to benefits along our paths - either **the mind** or **the heart**.

What tools does the mind have as a guide to our benefits?

The mind is very good at setting goals- we can move in this direction. There is also such a tool as checklists - you can create special motivational elements for yourself. You can also search for measurable results - try something, compare, and evaluate. You are probably familiar with such a tool as a "Wish Map" (visualization on paper), and in an updated version (we will talk about this below), it can be quite interesting. The mind does all this. Thus, our path to benefits can indeed be very logical and meaningful.

The mind leads us by logic - always on a linear path, and this is a linear movement towards benefits.

And what about the heart?

The path of the heart is voluminous and non-linear, and it does not give step-by-step instructions. The heart has a completely different set of tools to communicate with us:

Firstly, it is a feeling through a state.

Secondly, it is a sixth sense.

Thirdly, it is an inner observer - the ability to observe oneself is already a great benefit. One more point - higher meanings: when we talk about our benefits and at the same time think about higher meanings, then naturally here we listen to our heart.

So, there are **two main paths**: **the mind** and **the heart**. The mind has a linear path; the heart has a voluminous, quantum path.

Which is better?

You know the right answer: **the best path is the path of balancing** these two components, the ability to move along two paths simultaneously. Here, it is very important to understand that each one works on these paths.

For example, what work does the Matrix do? The Matrix "looks at us" 24/7 and constantly offers us various things for our benefit - in general, this is its task: to offer us these benefits, and it works by the method of resonance - it offers us those benefits that resonate with us.

If we constantly see around us an offer to buy a new house, then with a high probability we can say that this topic is of interest to us now and we are thinking about it. If you've noticed, as soon as you think about searching for some thing or object, the Internet immediately throws up options for us.

This is how quantum reality works: Advanced marketing and advertising campaigns work on this principle - it's enough to find one site or click on one advertisement on a topic, and similar ads immediately pour in on us - the Matrix shows and offers us exactly what we want inside, to what benefits we are moving, and accordingly, among the whole set of what the Matrix offers, the main part is temptation. The Matrix's goal is not at all to give us a benefit so that we can buy a plot for seven generations in the cemetery. The Matrix is initially focused on the task of our stay here on Earth, and it is not at all connected with the material.

The non-material benefit for which we are here is experience. The passage and living through experience is what happens inside us. Any external benefits are a tool for activating this experience, a tool for its passage, and nothing more. When we remember this main semantic content of our stay on Earth, many things fall into place, such as why the Matrix gives so many temptations.

We have a great chance to distinguish between what we need and what is just an empty temptation, and if I don't need it, I have the free will not to get involved in this temptation. I can stop at any moment and say: "No, thank you, I don't need it." This is how you can stop any flow: be it intrusive offers, no matter how tempting, any negative information - all this can be stopped by one's own pure intention and clear choice.

To determine what benefits I need and how to get to them in the shortest way, it is very important to understand that imbalances happen on this path, and, as we know, life itself is balancing. Therefore, if we are pulled into the material, it is normal. The main thing is to turn on the observer in time, track this moment, and balance the "flight." There is an imbalance in the so-called "spirituality".

We all know such a concept as fanaticism, when people get hung up on some illusions, move away from the reality of this day and moment, cease to be attentive to their body, their life, their loved ones, their responsibilities, and begin to euphorically "fanatic" about some non-material benefits, and this is also an imbalance.

In the modern world, imbalance in the pursuit of benefits is common, so if we are unbalanced, we turn on the observer and balance ourselves. And when we are on the middle path, on a balanced path to our benefits, to their receipt, we naturally begin to treat them healthily and adequately.

"MINE - NOT MINE" TEST

Please relax. Now is N.E.O.Pause

I suggest you do right now

a N.E.O.Pause-test - "Beneficial state."

We will go through a simple inner awareness test. We will enter a state from which you will feel you really desire your benefit and understand whether it is the benefit you need or it is not the benefit at all, and it is suggested to you, for example, by the Matrix, society, or some stereotypes.

You can also use this method to test habits to determine whether or not you need a particular habit.

Read the instructions and then do the exercise.

I ask you to choose any benefit that you wish for yourself. It can be any object, it can be some kind of trip, it can be relationships - manifest what you want. Try to formulate it enough to create a thought form.

Sit up straight, straighten your shoulders, your back is straight. Smile, close your eyes, take a breath and exhale. A few seconds of attention to the breath.

And now we manifest on the screen of the inner observer the benefit that we wish to embody in our life. Imagine it right in front of you, from your spiritual heart; stretch a ray into this picture. And now enter into it.

You are inside the picture.

If it is an object, you are holding it in your hands or are in it (for example, in a car). If it is a relationship, you see a partner holding their hand; if it is a trip, you are inside this picture.

Breathe, feel your state. Is it gracious, or is the mind fussing? Breathe.

Come back to yourself. Return the ray to the center of the heart.

Smile and open your eyes.

If you find yourself in a gracious state inside your desire or habit that you are testing, then it means that you need it; boldly go there.

And if you were constantly thinking: right hand or left hand, oh, is it this way or not, and how is it better, and all the time your mind was on, then most likely, this is not the benefit or not the habit that you need.

Try to study your desire more deeply and how it came to you. Remember where you learned that you could want this. From an advertising campaign? After all, even in relationships, people often have a very imaginary idea of how exactly they should develop.

Of course, kind, wonderful relationships with a partner are a benefit, and many would like to receive such a benefit, but not everyone needs it. Yes, we are guided by beliefs instilled in us from childhood that everyone should be in pairs, but at different stages of life, it happens in different ways, in different lives in different ways. Some come here to go on the path of loneliness. Our event series are manifested for us precisely for those tasks with which we came here.

In order not to waste energy in vain, try to test your desires and habits with the help of such a simple N.E.O.Pause and feel your state inside an already realized desire or developed habit. How do you feel: gracious or not? If you are in benefit - go ahead to realization. If the mind controls, it is desirable to work on this more so as not to waste energy in vain on obtaining benefits that do not please later, which happens very often.

Example:

Surely, you know people whose material Well-Being is very high, but at the same time, they are not left by inner anxiety, discomfort, worry, or mental anguish. They may even seek solace in alcohol and drugs but do not find it. What is it? This is an imbalance towards material benefits.

People having a large amount of money, can afford a lot while often not distinguishing what they need and what is a tribute to fashion, prestige, status, or simply the confusion of conventions imposed by the consumer society. They immerse themselves increasingly in accumulating material goods, which only contributes to an even greater imbalance and, hence, emptiness.

The same is true in reverse: people who fanatically reject the material benefits that civilization provides us, over the years, become eternally dissatisfied grumblers, too harsh and too principled, lose heartiness, and this is also a rejection of balance.

The choice they made themselves at one time, over the years, led them to such an imbalance, so it is very important on the path to receiving benefits to keep in balance - to check: what I want constantly, are these my benefits, or are they suggested to me.

GRATITUDE IS A TOOL OF COSMIC SCALE

I am for Well-Being. Well-Being is the process of receiving benefits, including the meanings in which it is offered to us by the current level of development of our civilization. I am for us to use the highest quality products of our civilization, but to use them with an eco-approach - ecologically.

When we move along the path of a balanced receipt of benefits - Well-Being - we understand that the first and main basis for benefit-receiving is **benefit-giving, gratitude**.

If something is wrong with benefits in your life, and you feel that from the point of view of balance, you are doing well - that is, you clearly understand what material benefits you need and understand the non-material benefits that are important to you - but there are no benefits, pay attention to benefit-giving.

Where and how do you give benefits? We remember that in the quantum world, 1+1 equals 11. The more we give, the more we receive. This does not mean at all that you need to give everything away. Let's not forget about balance. When we reflect on benefit-giving, we begin to look for where and to whom we can say Thank you. And we do this even before we start thinking about who we can give what to, give away, give as a gift.

We begin to be grateful to give benefits, and benefits begin to happen. This is the very first and most reliable method after you have placed yourself at the point of a balanced awareness of the benefits you need.

Giving must be based on purity of intention. You cannot be grateful not from a pure heart. The point is not to write dithyrambs on three sheets in small handwriting. You can write one phrase or say one word, but do it from such a depth of sincerity of your heart that it will be counted as three volumes.

Please relax. Now is N.E.O.Pause

And now I suggest you do an **N.E.O.Pause of Gratitude**.

Read the description of the technique below and do it right away without putting it off for later.

It will take 3 minutes;
It will bring a tangible effect;
Check it yourself in practice.

We take a comfortable position, straighten the back, and straighten the shoulders so that they do not constrain the rib cage through which air moves. We take a slow breath all the way to the bottom of the abdomen and smoothly exhale. Breathing is the most important tool in any N.E.O.Pause. We close our eyes and begin to breathe consciously: this means we observe how the inhalation occurs, and we do not interfere with it, and how the exhalation occurs, and again, we do not interfere.

I take the position of an observer and observe my breathing with my inner gaze, and I feel how relaxation spreads throughout the body from breathing. The body relaxes even more from this. The back straightens even more. I will imagine and stretch a light string along the spine consciously. The shoulders are straightened, and everything is fine. Politely, with pure intention, I will tell my brain to stop the chatter. Now is the time for me, for immersion in my silence.

I observe my breathing and shift my attention to the center of the chest. With intention, I allow myself to shine. The light of my heart spreads in waves, radially, in all directions, fills my entire physical body, and synchronizes with every cell of my body. Light fills the head, shoulders, arms, chest, abdomen, back, and legs. Touching the feet, my attention indicates what my feet are touching now: socks, floor, carpet, shoes. The light of my heart spreads without borders, forward without borders, left *without borders, and right without borders, in all directions between them, down without borders, and up without borders.*

I will pull a light string again, straighten my axis even more, and straighten my shoulders. I breathe, shine, smile, rejoice. Everything is fine.

I will say clearly and distinctly aloud or to myself: I thank the Higher forces of creation for this, I thank the love and light flowing through me, I thank Life, I thank Mother Earth, the Sun, the stars, our entire Galaxy. Add your own gratitude. I thank myself for doing this N.E.O.Pause and thereby joining the infinite source of life energy. I am grateful; I will smile and open my eyes.

PURITY OF INTENTIONS ON THE PATH TO WELL-BEING IS THE KEY

Whatever we do: whether we want or give benefits - the key must be in this lock: pure intention.

Pure intention is when there are no otherworldly thoughts of gain, no double bottom, and no expectations, especially when you are grateful and give benefits. And when this is done with pure intention, every person feels it: the one who receives and the one who gives. Therefore, if someone tells you thank you from a pure heart, you instantly feel it because pure intention refers to non-verbal communication.

And in exactly the same way, when you sincerely thank, the person will feel it.

This is already the heartfelt side of the question, this is when we, with the help of activating our heart, allowing ourselves to be and live in trust, begin to give, and then benefits come to us.

The key word is trust. Trust characterizes the path of the heart to benefit-receiving, that is, Well-Being.

TRUST AND EASE

Let's dwell in more detail on this important topic for Well-Being - the topic of **trust**.

Trust in life as such is the best guide on the path to benefit-receiving Well-Being.

Our mind constantly invites us to temptations and builds such clear, logical chains and constructions that it is very difficult to resist them. And here, the state of trust comes to the rescue.

Do I trust the Universe if the benefit I strive for does not come into my hands? Of course, you can go head-on and bend everything and everyone, still achieve what you want along the way, wasting a lot of energy and resources, and, upon receiving what you want, not feel joy. But you can trust the world and let go, at least for a while, of those desires that are not yet being fulfilled.

If you want to buy a house, but it does not come, try to trust life. Perhaps you do not need this house; maybe the universe has other plans for you, or maybe a better house option exists.

The same is true with any other material thing or benefits we think we desire. If you have already figured out that you keep a good balance, you have checked with the help of the N.E.O.Pause that this benefit is exactly what you want, you have already done the N.E.O.Gratitude Practice, that is, you have begun to give more, and more good gifts to the outside world, and what you desire still does not happen, then relax and trust the Universe. When you really need this benefit in your purity and sincerity, it will definitely appear in your life and in all its glory, not in half measures and not in compromises.

SIMPLE SIGNS OF A TRUSTING LIFE PATH

Very often, trust is replaced by logic, and it substitutes meanings. I want to share one simple way to find out if we really stay in trust in life, that it has not gone anywhere, and that we have not tilted to the side of logic while under the illusion of our complete trust.

How to find out?

There are several signs:

First is **surprise**: when we have not lost the ability to be surprised sincerely. The logical mind is not surprised. It sees a phenomenon, immediately classifies it, and arranges it on the shelves. And if we are sincerely surprised, it means that we live in trust in life. If you have common childlike amazement at life in its everyday life, then you live in trust, which means that it is not difficult for you to understand your true benefits, and the paths to them will be much shorter.

The second indicator is **joy** in the soul for no reason. **Quiet, calm joy as a background state is a sign of the right, trusting attitude to life.** Feeling joy just like that, without any reason, is the most correct and natural human condition.

There is one more characteristic sign - **peacefulness**. If a person lives in trust in life, then they are a peace-loving person, and they are kind-hearted. Peace-loving does not mean that they are weak-willed, naive, foolish, or some kind of "nerd" or weakling. They can be deeply intelligent and highly educated, large-scale, physically strong... anything, and simultaneously kind-hearted. And this **kind-heartedness is a sign of trust in life**.

And one more sign is **the desire to communicate with people**. If we are open to communicating with people, this is also a sign of trust. Remember how children live in complete trust in the world, how easily they get acquainted and enter into contact with other children, how they show curiosity and surprise. Such a joyful, childlike component within our vibrations is about trust.

These are such signs, and if these signs are yours, then you live in trust in life, which means that the benefits that you wish for yourself most often come to you easily, without effort. The unnecessary ones do not come. And you do not desire the unnecessary ones. You are in balance, in equilibrium between the material and the non-material. This is the shortest way to benefit when we realize all this in this way.

WHAT CAN YOU WISH FOR?

You can wish for anything; the limitations are only inside us. Any benefits - you can have everything. The only thing that is needed is to check them in a balanced way, do an N.E.O.Pause, feel yourself in this benefit, as if we had already received it, and determine whether it is ours.

Another very good tool is the "Map of Desires and Beneficial Habits." Many are probably already familiar with it, but I want to note that it can already be a quantum tool. If before we created these maps of desires materially - we cut out some pictures from magazines, pasted it all on a sheet of paper, and wrote down specific wishes, now we can do this practice with the help of N.E.O.Pauses - the way it is described above.

You can create a "Map of Desires and Beneficial Habits" or write a list of your desired benefits and Well-Being habits that you plan to establish. To help you, there is the N.E.O.Workbook for this book.

After that, enter the N.E.O.Pause-test - "Beneficial state" and feel the state inside each of these desires, live it through. It may happen that you will cancel half of the list already at this stage because you have already lived it through during practice, and you no longer want it, or at the moment, you realize that this is not your desire at all, but something inspired from the outside.

Our N.E.O.Home is an internal construction of all our fields, as well as our entire reality, united together, and with the help of visualization in the N.E.O.Pause, we can live our desire in test mode even before it is materialized - and this is a wonderful opportunity of modern energies - to do this practice in your N.E.O.Home.

SPIRITUAL MATURITY OF DESIRES

When we go along the path of receiving our benefits, it is necessary to take into account an important detail: this is **the level (or Floor) of Awareness** at which we want to receive these benefits.

What does this mean?

The first thing to say is the **scale of values**. If the scale of our values is too materialized, then, naturally, we will always want material benefits, and this will grow in progression. Desires will arise one after another on an expanding scale: if you want a car - you got a car, you realized that it's not it..., you want a better car, then you want a lot of cars. I know people with a whole fleet of cars; they don't even have time to ride some cars once a year, and this does not fill them. Because the settings of the scale of values are lost, precisely this lies at the basis of Well-Being.

The second component is **reasonable sufficiency**. This is precisely the balance point when I understand that my material and non-material desires are adequate.

Now let's remember that space is not linear; space is voluminous quantum, a pyramid, and we are in the Pyramid - in the Pyramid of Human Uniqueness©[1], we are unique. [1]Our point in the

---

[1] (The Pyramid of Human Uniqueness by Contoret© – an indicator of a person's spiritual maturity. See Glossary.)

Pyramid© (Floor in the Pyramid©) is where we are at the moment. It is important to understand on what Floor in the Pyramid of Awareness© my desire is, my balance, the balance of my desires, where this point is.

What if awareness rises? How do my desires change? A lot. Very much. The higher the Floor in the Pyramid©, the fewer desires we have. Neale Donald Walsch said this well when he was asked, "Tell me, how can you measure awareness?" He replied very beautifully: "I measure my awareness by the number of my desires, the amount of what I need for happiness." The more a person is aware, the higher their Floor in the Pyramid©, and the fewer desires they have because the more a person is happy from the inside, the less they seek happiness from the outside, and the more happiness a person has inside, the more benefits they can give, and accordingly, then also benefit-receive.

Well-Being comes to an absolute state of lightness and instantness, firstly, because you don't need much, and secondly, because the path is pure, from pure intentions.

CHAPTER 5.
12 FOUNDATIONS OF WELL-BEING — HOW TO CREATE YOUR ABUNDANT REALITY

Here, we will talk about a prosperous life. In order for life to be prosperous, it is necessary to take care of it.

Does life happen to be prosperous by itself? Yes, it does, but if we have already taken care of it - in a past life, for example. And if we see that in our hectic time, the balance that we build inside ourselves with such attention and respect is very quickly disturbed due to external turbulent processes, then we understand that caring for Well-Being becomes an ordinary everyday process when we send our attention exactly where the need arises, to maintain inner balance, inner equilibrium.

So, let's take care of our Well-Being. When I say, let's take care of the Well-Being; then here you need to understand that the focus of our attention in this matter should be directed exclusively at ourselves. The entrance door to a prosperous life is to be a priority for yourself, first of all, to take care of yourself.

Let's note subtly here that caring for yourself taking care of yourself is the work of the soul, but the concern is the fuss of the brain, so we do not confuse these two concepts, and we always carefully relate to whether we are taking care of ourselves or we are concerned about ourselves. Now that we have understood the meaning of these two similar words, but with different semantic meanings, let's focus on genuine self-care, which means taking care of our Well-Being.

From my life experience, I have derived 12 main areas of self-care, and I want to share them with you.

1ST, SELF-CARE IS TAKING CARE OF YOUR MENTAL BALANCE

What do you need to do for this? For this, it is very important not to take on more than the psyche can allow us at a particular moment without violating the homeostasis of its inner space, which means not getting involved in any processes that take away our energy in surges or with strong involvement. These can be both external and internal processes if they have a bright emotional coloring, that is, experiences that cause a loss of energy.

We take care of ourselves so that our psyche is in balance.

On the one hand, we do not get involved: we do not watch TV, scroll through news feeds, or turn on the TV in the background at night for sleep under any circumstances.

On the other hand, we regularly allow ourselves relaxation, spa, wellness therapies, and healthy nutrition. And then our psyche is compensated within itself; it is not very much wasted and is all the time structured by conscious actions - this is a very important care because when our psyche is in order, balanced, and in equilibrium, then we can be 100% sure that we will be able to easily and with pleasure perform all other cares in everyday life.

CARE NO. 2 IS TAKING CARE OF YOUR SPINE

The spine is undoubtedly the channel through which energy moves. It is the axis that holds the physical body and the entire set of field structures of our N.E.O.Home, so here it is very important to learn the correct operation: to get out of bed correctly, to sleep on a good mattress and a good pillow; to sit on comfortable chairs; to do joint and muscle gymnastics; to competently alternate load and relaxation.

CARE NO. 3 IS TAKING CARE OF BODY FLEXIBILITY

It is interesting that flexibility also indicates how balanced we are inside, relaxed, and in harmony. If your body is flexible, if you easily touch the floor with your hands, if you easily take different figures or sit and sit for a sufficiently long time in the lotus position, then this is a very good indicator. If this does not happen to you, then be sure to include elements of yoga, work with the feet, gymnastics, and stretching in your daily rhythm of life. It can be yoga and Pilates, dance elements, or anything that contributes to increasing your body's flexibility, and this quality should improve from day to day and from year to year.

It is a mistake to think that flexibility decreases with age. Not at all. My personal experience shows that with daily simple but systematic conscious warm-ups and training, body flexibility not only does not decrease with age but even increases.

4TH CARE IS TAKING CARE OF THE SKIN AND HAIR

Hair is our antenna; they perceive energy they conduct it, so the hair should be in order: combed, not tangled, clean. The skin is the boundary between our physical shell and the environment and can indicate the harmony of relationships with the outside world.

We carefully monitor how our skin feels and pay attention to symptoms - if there are any manifestations on the skin, this may be a signal that we have lost harmony somewhere.

Do not forget about facial gymnastics.

We raise the standard of quality of our care from year to year.

5TH CARE IS TAKING CARE OF RELATIONSHIPS

If you noticed, the first four cares would relate to the psycho-physical aspect: mental balance plus three bodily cares - the spine, flexibility, skin, and hair. This is because we are constantly in illusions without maintaining this wonderful foundation of balance. We can build superstructures as much as we want, but without a stable base, they will constantly crumble, so for care number five, about relationships, it is very important that care for your body is compensated and becomes the norm of life.

What does it mean to take care of relationships? Relationships should be comfortable, harmonious, and balanced in the give/take theme. They should increase joy. If there are non-working relationships - deficient, causing suffering, taking away energy, then it is imperative to look inside. Relationships need to be tuned like any mechanism, so caring for kind, happy, comfortable relationships is our everyday work. You don't need to do it all at once or in surges, rush, or push, but it is very important to do it systematically. And even more importantly - do not tolerate relationships that destroy you.

6TH CARE IS TAKING CARE OF THE PURITY OF YOUR VIBRATIONS

Our outer space is a mirror, so everything that happens in our life in the event series mirrors what happens inside us and what vibration we emit into this world. As the Master says: "What we radiate is what we get."

If the space around you is pure: pure people, pure relationships, clear situations, then it means that your inner space vibrates wonderfully, it is pure, and the frequency of these vibrations is favorable and prosperous. And if we talk about purity literally, then this is already.

CARE NO. 7, AND HERE WE ARE TALKING ABOUT PURITY IN ITS USUAL SENSE

It is imperative to take care of the cleanliness of your space - home, your clothes, your speech, the purity of your choices, and the purity of your intentions. When we consciously clean the inner space and outer space, and we can say: my N.E.O.Home is clean, then at the same moment, life itself rebuilds into an event series of Well-Being.

CARE NO. 8 IS TAKING CARE OF JOY AND EASE

Joy is a field; joy is a state. When we radiate joy, then the field structure, this beautiful Torus, this torsion field - by itself harmonizes all processes and events in our life into Well-Being.

Ease, joy, good mood, interest, meanings of life - all this is very important. That is the reason.

CARE NO. 9 IS TAKING CARE OF MEANINGS

Meanings can be earthly, or they can be stellar.

In endless vanity, meanings are not visible.

Some people condemn themselves to the meanings of completely primitive levels, such as serving exclusively their family or work - something narrowly focused. In this way, a person closes themselves off.

It is very important to raise your head and think about your stellar meanings: Why did I come into this life, to this Earth? What exactly do I want to understand, learn, and realize here? What meanings did I see from there before the incarnation?

In order to see these meanings, daily practices and meditations are absolutely necessary, and all 12 cares are necessary, then these meanings suddenly open up by themselves.

10TH CARE IS TAKING CARE OF MOVING FORWARD

Changes, new things, discovery, learning. It is very important not to stagnate in life. Constant movement is necessary. Therefore, if you feel that everything around you has somehow settled and become monotonous every day, fix it.

Move forward, and do it with pure intention.

CARE NO. 11 IS TAKING CARE OF BEAUTY AND PLEASANTNESS FOR THE FIVE SENSES

We are in this body and have the wonderful opportunity to perceive and know this world with the help of our five senses. Take care that it is beautiful and pleasant at the level of all five senses.

Go to beautiful places, and take care that your eyes see beautiful things in your home, coziness, cleanliness, surroundings, design, decor, and flowers. Go for walks in beautiful places, communicate with beautiful people, dress beautifully, and be sure to take care of your reflection in the mirror - do you like yourself?

Do not forget that the beauty that we perceive through sight puts beautiful pictures in our subconscious, from which the subconscious creates our future. Do not forget that delicious food should also be aesthetically and beautifully served and that good smells are very important to us for our Care No. 1 about the psyche. Do not forget that touching pleasant quality things is a pleasure and pleasantness; take care of this, too - tactile pleasures are also very necessary.

CARE NO. 12 IS TAKING CARE OF FINANCIAL AND MATERIAL SUFFICIENCY

It is not for nothing that I have put this care in 12th place. Nevertheless, it is among the main cares for a prosperous life. Why at the very end? I observe the tendency for everyone to think about finances as care number one, which is a mistake. When we start with care from number one - from the psyche - and reach the eleventh - about beauty and pleasantness, then already by the twelfth point, we realize that we are more or less balanced in finance and material sufficiency.

Nevertheless, care for this should be the focus of attention.

Here is a good rule: reasonable sufficiency on one side, and on the other side, not getting involved in energy-consuming activities such as loan debt obligations.

Put your affairs and finances in order. Do not forget to set aside a reserve fund for yourself, for example, 10%, which you invest once a year: perhaps you will need it for a vacation; perhaps you will decide to buy some interesting course for development; perhaps your children will need some additional finances in a couple of years, and you will use this reserve for this.

The reserve fund is a fund that the family or the person creates for themselves - in fact, it directly closes the circle with Care No. 1 - about mental balance. When, at the level of the subconscious, we understand that we have something to rely on materially, and in case of any unexpected situations, we know that there is a certain reasonable and sufficient supply of finances or some investments that can be immediately used for this, then our psyche is really in balance.

The energy of money is very strong - many underestimate it. It is very important to understand that the society in which we live is materially oriented, and every day, we hear conversations about money from various sources, from people around us, so the psyche at all levels of the subconscious absorbs it even deeper into itself and reacts to it. The financial issue must be closed with sufficient reasonableness and in reasonable sufficiency to balance the psyche.

All these 12 self-cares are easiest **to introduce into your life without tension with the help of Well-Being habits**. It is Well-Being habits that are aimed at making self-care a habitual, natural thing in the life of each of us.

CHAPTER 6.
THREE LIVE N.E.O.SKILLS OF WELL-BEING

What competencies do we need in modern life? Skills have always been necessary for humanity, and at all times, people have nurtured, created, and developed them in themselves.

It is known that creating a skill requires attention and discipline. But times have changed, and we need new skills. What exactly are they, and how do people relate to skills in general?

A skill can also be something like a template that hinders us, limits us, and holds us back. Like when we, like trolleys, ride on rails and cannot turn off this track.

But there are also useful skills - those that help us live. For example, there is the skill of always walking with a straight back. Not only walking, sitting - just living with a straight back. If I did not acquire this skill in childhood, then in adulthood, I will need much more effort to create this habit for myself, and it will be a skill of a healthy lifestyle. Daily, we need healthy, live skills that transform this life into Well-Being.

These three live skills serve as global platforms for the process of developing beneficial habits. We will analyze what these skills are and why they are needed.

So, three live N.E.O.Skills:

- **The skill of good mood**
- **The skill of healthy eating**
- **The skill of self-care**

These are the simple skills we need in the modern world. They will be absolutely necessary for us in the new time. The new planetary energies that the Earth is now welcoming from the entire Universe are combined into such wonderful isofractals in which these three skills will help us automatically fit into the new rhythms of life and live prosperously.

Some of you may say: I already always have a good mood, eat healthy and take care of myself. But we will work on these live skills in a slightly new way because we will explore the question: Why do we need these skills?

THE FIRST SKILL IS A GOOD MOOD.

What is the skill of a good mood? It is not some kind of discipline that exists naturally by itself. No. It is the work of the soul. The soul understands that the skill of a good mood provides joy, and joy is a manifestation of inner harmony. On joy, as on a special fuel, humanity is now moving forward towards its future.

Our inner harmony, the state of quiet, calm joy inside - creates a certain vibration, and this vibration has the property of transmitting and attracting. By radiating the vibration of a good mood, we automatically spread it around us, to our family, loved ones, and everyone we communicate with, and at the same time, vibrating at the frequency of a good mood, joy, we attract from the quantum space the same people, with the same mood, we attract events that are born in joy, and all this fits into our event branches and creates a natural prosperous reality.

There is one more very important point in understanding why we need to be in a good mood. The state of joy in which we stay completely works in a new way biochemically with our inner space - with the cell itself. When a cell vibrates at the frequency of joy, it is open to the flow of living life energy. That is why it is so important for us to stay in a state of joy.

In fact, we are just maintaining a good mood but doing it quite consciously and working on it. When we have succeeded in this skill, we automatically begin to maintain our good mood, the flow of living energy, prosperous life events, and good relationships with people - because we radially give this joy - all this happens by itself, it seems by itself. But this complex algorithm works only on the fuel of joy. And for this we need a good mood.

THE SECOND SKILL IS HEALTHY EATING.

Why is it so important now?

Firstly, the balanced biochemical environment of our body in exactly the same way contributes to the direct flow of the life energy of Zhiva through us into our cells, into our space, and organizes our

N.E.O.Home, the system of our fields. And this is also, albeit invisibly to us, an absolutely important foundation for us to resonate with space on the purity of joy.

Secondly, if we eat healthy food, we do not waste energy on energy-consuming digestion. Many think healthy eating is boiling pasta and dumping a can of canned peas or corn into it. This is not so. Energetically, such food is not healthy at all. We are talking about healthy eating in terms of our energies, so healthy eating will never overload our body and will not take a lot of energy for complex digestion.

The third reason we need this skill is that healthy food transforms into life energy, into high-quality life energy, and all this together is a serious foundation for a prosperous and healthy life.

THE THIRD SKILL IS THE SKILL OF SELF-CARE.

Of course, it is very important to remember that this is not self-care from an ego position. **This is the N.E.O.Position of self-care: I am a priority for myself** because my energy resource allows me to distribute energy around. That's why it's important to be a priority for yourself. That is why it is important with the help of N.E.O.Practices, N.E.O.Pauses to learn a new skill to take care of yourself and your energy during the day.

Sufficiency of life energy in any event manifestations provides confidence that I will not go out of myself, I will not go out of my

N.E.O.Home, I will remain myself, I will remain, no matter what happens. I have a lot of energy and will not be drawn into an emotional funnel; nothing will disturb my balance. That is why, when we are in such a resource, we are absolutely energy-sufficient for ourselves and our loved ones.

An important reason we need to have the skill of self-care is that we conduct light through ourselves. We are entities that live on light energy, and we came to this planet to be conductors of light. For this light to flow and pass through us unhindered, our resources must be sufficient so that the incoming light is not blocked by shortcomings, compromises, blocks, and some darkening in our fields.

That is why these three live N.E.O.Skills are the foundation of a prosperous life in our time. Why are these live skills? Because they need to be lived through. Live skills create our reality with you, our prosperous life with you, so they are transformed. For each of us, the creation of such a skill will proceed in a peculiar, unique way.

HOW DOES LIFE CHANGE WITH LIVE SKILLS?

Imagine that you have three such wonderful skills.

Life will change completely.

Let's assume how life will change if we have the skill of a good mood - life becomes joyful. Living in joy is what each of us wants to have.

How will life change if we have the skill of healthy eating - life will be with good health. It will not just be good, it will also be motivating because it will also allow us to help our loved ones switch to healthy eating and apply this skill.

Well, if we have the skill of caring for ourselves, what will happen? First of all, what will happen is that our main life relationships will be absolutely adjusted - these are relationships with ourselves. And as you know, by improving our relationships with ourselves, we improve them with everyone around us. A person in harmony with himself has no conflicts with people; non-conflicting people are attracted to him. That is the skill of self-care. The living N.E.O.Skill will form harmonious relationships around you.

Imagine you have a life of joy, good health, and harmonious relationships.

This is it, a prosperous life.

Well-Being is an applied value. But habits are a practice, so that we will create them all together.

CHAPTER 7. CATALOG OF 100 MICRO HABITS FOR MEGA WELL-BEING

We offer you **a catalog of 100 habits** for a Prosperous life in its ten spheres:

MOOD

THOUGHTS

SPEECH

BODY

FOOD

RELATIONSHIPS

HOUSEKEEPING (EVERYDAY LIFE)

TRAVEL

RHYTHM

MONEY

1ST SPHERE. MOOD

Habit No.1. Make it a habit to decide on your own mood.

- No one and nothing can spoil your mood if you don't agree to it.

- Manage your emotions with love.

Habit No.2. Easily smooth out mood swings with affirmations without outside help.

- When you notice a mood swing, read an affirmation out loud to yourself.
- Come up with affirmations for yourself that make you smile.
  - I am cheerful, full of glee; all my deeds go well for me.
  - Life has blessed me with its glow—things resolve themselves.

Habit No.3. Love your emotions and manage them.

- Emotions affect mood.
- Check and filter the sources of emotions - news, TV, conversations.

Habit No.4. In the pace of your life, stop for short N.E.O.Pauses several times a day.

- Micro-practice does not take time or disrupt plans but gives energy.
- The key to a good mood tomorrow is the proper completion of affairs today - do an N.E.O.Pause at night, too.

Habit No.5. Create a priority for yourself to live in a good mood.

- A good mood is a marker of a sufficient amount of life energy. Maintain your energy level throughout the day consciously.

- A changeable mood indicates an unstable, resourceful state in your field. Find the source of energy leakage in yourself and eliminate it.

Habit No.6. Don't eat sweets when you're in a bad mood.

- If your mood is spoiled, do something else and shift your attention to what makes you happy.
- Drink a glass of warm water or tea - this will help relieve tension in the body.

Habit No.7. Share your good mood.

- Mood is transmitted from person to person. Consciously keep your mood high and pass it on.
- A good mood can be given or received as a gift through a smile, a compliment, or a kind word.

Habit No.8. Elegantly minimize communication with toxic people.

- You don't need boring, complaining, and dissatisfied people!
- And if these are people from your close circle, then limit interaction to a sufficient minimum.

Habit No.9. Allow yourself to live for your pleasure.

- Healthy and beautiful food in the company of people you like perfectly raises your mood.
- Give yourself joy and pleasure - it always works.

Habit No.10. Smile with pleasure.

- A smile is the key to lifting your mood.

- Smile to yourself, to yourself in the mirror, and to people.

2ND SPHERE. THOUGHTS

Habit No.1. Observe your thoughts with love.

- Get rid of other people's thoughts in your head - 90% of them are not yours.
- Do the N.E.O.Pause "Clear Head": "I free/clear my head from alien programs and other people's thoughts." (*Find a detailed description in the* N.E.O.*Workbook*).

Habit No.2. Stop the inner dialogue.

- Form the habit of stopping the chatter in your head: change your focus of attention or type of activity.
- Don't get drawn into the funnel of internal discussions, and energy drains into it like into a hole.

Habit No.3. Think voluminously and dream big.

- The scale of thinking defines a person.
- Travel learns new things - it expands the boundaries of perception and trains the ability to say "yes" to the world.

Habit No.4. Think easily.

- LightThinking is a high quality of the soul. Develop it in yourself, and do not confuse it with irresponsibility.
- LightThinking is the opposite of sluggish thinking.

Habit No.5. Think and speak with dignity.

- Think and speak from a state of dignity. This will relieve your speech of unnecessary phrases and excuses and allow you to agree in peace.
- Everything in this world is worthy of your calmness.

Habit No.6. Learn to express your thoughts in a structured way.

- In business relationships, think clearly and to the point. Leave everything else for romantic relationships.
- Don't jump from fifth to tenth when you speak. Hold the thread of your thought.

Habit No.7. Keep your thoughts clean.

- Thoughts are like living water - they form your reality. Don't spill them in vain; develop the need to stop bad thoughts and keep thoughts clean.

Habit No.8. Express your thoughts clearly.

- Develop the ability to clearly and simply express your thoughts and intentions. This will simplify all relationships and eliminate misunderstandings with family and loved ones.
- Everything that is simple is for growth; everything that is complex is false.

Habit No.9. Think positively and lightly.

- Thought is the basis of creating reality. Cherish and develop bright thoughts, and they are the source of a happy life.

- Positive thinking must be sincere, and then it works.

Habit No.10. Observe safety techniques in thinking and desires.

- Be attentive and careful in your desires, they come true.
- Bad and dark thoughts take away energy and lead to crooked paths. Get rid of them or transform them.

3RD SPHERE. SPEECH

Habit No.1. Keep your Speech clean.

- This will ensure purity in thoughts, intentions, and relationships.
- The fewer filler words in your speech, the easier it is for Well-Being to fill your Life.

Habit No.2. Exclude destructive words from your speech.

- For example, the destructive word PROBLEM - replace it with the words situation or task. Just think about it: this word sounds the same in all languages and is used everywhere. Why?
- Obscene and slang ugly words and expressions poison your energy.

Habit No.3. Be grateful always, everywhere, to everyone, for everything.

- Gratitude, when it comes from the heart, transforms the energy of your affairs and events into a Stream of Luck.

- Heartfelt gratitude heals.

Habit No.4. The ability to be silent and listen is the key to Well-Being.

- Listen to how a person speaks, and you will understand their thoughts. This will help you realize whether you can deal with them or not.
- The art of hearing is the ability to listen with the heart.

Habit No.5. Show politeness.

- Say hello and goodbye - even in the elevator. This creates a favorable vibration in the space where you are.
- Politeness as a habit opens many doors.

Habit No.6. Practice information unloading.

- Silence is golden. Sometimes have information unloading days or hours for yourself. Just be silent.
- Detoxing thoughts, desires, and aspirations is very useful and possible only in inner silence. Learn to do a 60-second N.E.O.Pause of "Silence". (*You will find a description of the practice in Chapter 9*).

Habit No.7. Show delicacy in your manner of speaking.

- Don't give advice that you weren't asked for. Beware of doing good harm.
- Develop your empathy, and delicacy grows easily and quickly from it.

Habit No.8. Be yourself: honest and sincere.

- Speak with your heart when you want to be convinced of your rightness and stand for it. Then, your words are helped by the vibration of the good qualities of your soul.
- Being honest and sincere is very simple and fantastically effective for any communication.

Habit No.9. Express yourself beautifully: elegantly, concisely, and competently.

- Expand your vocabulary to express your feelings, states, and wishes beautifully and deeply in the subtlest shades, no matter who you are talking to - a person or the Creator.
- Beautiful speech flows like a river.

Habit No.10. Be careful in communicating with people close and dear to you.

- Take care of your family and loved ones, and do not harm them with insults, verbal pressure, or a dissatisfied tone. The health of your loved ones is always reflected in your Well-Being.

4TH SPHERE. BODY

Habit No.1. Take care of your body in a versatile way.

- Your body is the place where you will stay until you change dimensions. Take care of it holistically - bones, muscles, skin, organs, teeth, hair. Also, create new neural connections, keep your mind sharp, and develop attentiveness.

Habit No.2. Move more: walk 10,000 steps a day.

- Even the Pope has this habit.
- There are many ways to walk: walk in the park, wander slowly barefoot on the grass, or it can be trekking in the mountains. Choose for yourself according to your soul.

Habit No.3. Do morning exercises, warm-ups, or stretching.

- It can be lying down, standing, sitting.
- Align your spine in the morning, and the energy channel along it will provide you with energy for the whole day.

Habit No.4. Use the rule of "3 waters in the morning":

- drink a glass of warm water
- warm up the body with movements until sweating
- take a shower/bath

Habit No.5. Create a habit of 3 N.E.O.Pauses of 5 minutes each day for the resourceful state of the body.

- The resourceful state is the basis of Well-Being and active longevity.
- These three N.E.O.Pauses work great:
    - breathing (we observe our breathing)
    - attentive (we focus our attention)
    - movement (we dance and jump for our pleasure)

Habit No.6. Thank your body for serving you.

- Bones, muscles, blood, eyes, heart, all internal organs, arms, and legs will gratefully respond to you with health.
- The energy of gratitude is healing energy. Heal yourself with a grateful thought or word.

Habit No.7. Perceive yourself holistically.

- BODY - SOUL - SPIRIT and CONSCIOUSNESS is a holistic system. If you want to unload your brain - go for a workout. If you want to restore your body health - start with your thoughts.
- The protein body has several levels of energy bodies, and they all cooperate.

Habit No.8. Listen to your body.

- Sensations in the body are sensors of the Creator's conversation with you. Listen to them and learn to read them.
- Uncomfortable sensations in the body or diseases signal a violation of the harmony of the energy space. If you don't pay attention to it, it will manifest in unpleasant events or destructive relationships.

Habit No.9. Move with dignity and keep your posture.

- Posture is the key to clear thinking, correct decisions, and right choices on the path to Well-Being.
- A straight back ensures a smooth flow of energy, which means health, joy, and lightness.

Habit No.10. When caring for the body, remember your multidimensionality.

- The protein body is a unique cosmic equipment for immersion in the density of earthly reality.
- It knows how to heal itself if you have high vibrations, a clean inner space, and good intentions.

5TH SPHERE. FOOD

Habit No.1. Drink before eating.

- Don't drink while eating or drink during meals.
- Drink a glass of non-cold water half an hour before eating.

Habit No.2. Notice and change your outdated eating habits to new useful ones.

- Consciously analyze your eating habits and replace those that are outdated.
- Replacing unnecessary habits with new ones is an effective practice in self-development.
- Eating habits change with age, geographic location, and lifestyle.

Habit No.3. Eat beautifully.

- An English proverb: If you want to eat at the queen's reception like at home, then eat at home like at the queen's reception.
- Beautiful food consists of aesthetic serving, quality dishes, and utensils pleasing to the eye.

Habit No.4. Thank your food before eating and drink before drinking.

- The N.E.O.Pause of gratitude before eating is an age-old tradition among all peoples.
- Say thanks out loud, holding hands.

Habit No.5. Eat in silence and tranquility without haste.

- Do not combine news feeds, stressful movies, and negative information with eating.
- Turning on pleasant music is useful
- A pleasant, leisurely conversation is an aid to digestion.

Habit No.6. Don't eat just anything.

- An exhortation from the famous Persian philosopher Omar Khayyam:

    To wisely live your life, you don't need much;
    Just stay calm and bear in mind two things:
    Better starve than eat whatever,
    And better be alone than with whoever.

Habit No.7. Try new dishes experiment.

- The world is full of delicious food; don't be afraid to try.
- The more varied your diet, the larger your neural network. Food develops us.

Habit No.8. Don't overeat.

- Observe reasonable sufficiency and pleasant aesthetics in food.

- If you are overeating due to stress, realize it and stop.

Habit No.9. Eat food that is good for you.

- Food is energy, like refueling. "Don't refuel with diesel - you will go like a tractor in the field."
- To implement high ideas, eat healthy and wholesome food to fly like a rocket.

Habit No.10. Eat in cleanliness and with clean thoughts.

- Let your table be clean and tidy before and after eating.
- Immerse your attention in the food, don't think about extraneous things, then eating becomes an effective source of energy inflow.

6TH SPHERE. RELATIONSHIPS

Habit No.1. Listen carefully to your interlocutor/partner.

- Listen to your interlocutor partner; don't interrupt.
- Enter into communication with the intention to hear and understand.

Habit No.2. Smile when communicating.

- A smile is light and warmth, it melts ice.
- A smile evokes a smile.

Habit No.3. Observe your reaction in different situations.

- Pause if you see your impulsiveness or reactivity.
- The inner observer prevents scandals and misunderstandings.

Habit No.4. Transmit a kind-hearted attitude to the interlocutor.

- Exclude black humor teasing.
- An open heart and honesty are the foundation of worthy relationships.

Habit No.5. Don't speak ill of people.

- Speak of people only as you would like them to speak of you.
- Don't discuss people behind their backs.
- Don't condemn, and don't judge. You have things to do without it.

Habit No.6. Always be yourself.

- Be yourself in any relationship and under any circumstances.
- An English proverb says: "Stay true to yourself, come rain or shine," which means that no external circumstances should make you lose yourself.

Habit No.7. Convey your thoughts clearly and distinctly, as clearly and intelligibly as possible.

- This rule will protect you from misunderstandings that destroy relationships.
- However, remember that if you need to explain, you don't need to.

Habit No.8. Develop the ability to distinguish people.

- Enter into partnerships with a person from your floor of spiritual maturity.
- A Chinese proverb says: "A fish and a bird can love each other, but where will they live."
- It's joyful and pleasant where you are understood.

Habit No.9. Listen and heed your partner with your heart.

- Choose a partner with your heart, watching how your eyes, ears, and brain evaluate them.
- We are all different because we are unique. Be flexible, but don't betray yourself. Stand your ground, but don't push.

Habit No.10. End relationships harmoniously.

- When ending a relationship, consciously return to yourself the energy that you invested in this relationship. For this, the N.E.O.Practice "Ending Relationships" is good. (*If you'd like to learn more about this N.E.O.Practice, please feel free to email me at victoria@1234neo.com*).
- The harmonious ending of relationships reduces the time of painful experiences.

7TH SPHERE. HOUSEKEEPING (EVERYDAY LIFE)

Habit No.1. Neatly make the bed after sleeping.

- Do the N.E.O.Practice of conscious presence while making the bed. To do this, completely focus on the process and

smile when everything is ready. This will ensure order in the head and an inflow of life energy.
- Before making the bed, throw back the blanket and let it air out.

Habit No.2. Leave the kitchen sink clean at night.

- The mood is guaranteed to improve when you enter the kitchen in the morning, and it's clean there!
- We don't leave the energy of "yesterday" for "tomorrow."

Habit No.3. Do a deep cleaning twice a year.

- A deep cleaning is when we clean inside, under, behind, and on top of cabinets. Don't forget about the windows.
- Cleaning is the purification of space. A clean household space harmonizes with the inner space of your N.E.O.Home and lies at the basis of Well-Being.
- To maintain cleanliness: clean from top to bottom, from the corners to the center.

Habit No.4. Turn household chores into a mental and spiritual practice.

- Focus on what you are doing: cleaning, laundry, ironing, cooking food - any action when you do it attentively, is a source of life energy for you.
- Consciously play this N.E.O.Practice, smile at it, observe how your life becomes more prosperous and easier, and share it with the people around you.

Habit No.5. Keep your work or play area tidy.

- Order in the computer and on the desktop provide order in the head. You like people who have their heads in order, right? So you will be liked by the people around you.
- All energies work like a mirror: as outside, so inside, as inside, so outside.

Habit No.6. Declutter from time to time.

- Excess things and objects at home limit your space, both physical and life freedom. Declutter when you feel it's time!
- This is a great opportunity to give or pass on things you don't need to people who will be happy to have them.

Habit No.7. Look at the beautiful.

- The view from the window forms subconscious processes. Look at the beautiful!
- A well-maintained house, garden, plot, indoor plants, a harmonious interior, and household items that are pleasant to you are a source of your good mood and resourceful state.

Habit No.8. Harmonize your home through order in the closets.

- Fold clean and dry linen and clothes consciously: in stacks, drawers/organizers, shelves.
- Order in closets - kitchen, linen, work - is the energy base of order in life.

Habit No.9. Keep your car clean.

- A car is an extension of your space. Keep it clean and in good condition.
- Cleaning the car, like cleaning the apartment - as needed, but at least once a month.

Habit No.10. Synchronize the clocks.

- All clocks: on the wrist, at home, at the office, on the wall, floor, desk, in the car, on the yacht - everywhere you live and go, should show the correct exact time. This aligns the space-time lines and harmonizes your reality.
- Remove non-working clocks from the house or repair them.

8TH SPHERE. TRAVEL

Habit No.1. Travel with clean suitcases.

- After each trip, wash your suitcase. When you pack for the next one, you won't have to worry about it.
- Hotel staff pay attention to the appearance of the traveler and their luggage. Neat and clean suitcases are the key to a polite and attentive attitude towards you.

Habit No.2. Before traveling, sit "for the road."

- Why is this necessary? To remove anxiety, stop rushing, and tune in with joy to the trip.
- This N.E.O.Practice will take only three minutes and provide a good mood. To do this, sit down before leaving the house, close your eyes, and wish yourself a happy journey.

Habit No.3. Do check-in with a smile.

- Even if you do online check-in, smile anyway.
- Check-in with a smile at the airport or hotel will ensure the employee's loyalty to you, and you can get an upgrade or service bonus.

Habit No.4. Relieve your excitement while traveling.

- Consciously compensate for excitement with music, affirmations, and meditation.
- The breathing N.E.O.Pause "Angel Wings" helps great. 2-4 minutes - and calmness is restored. (*If you'd like to learn more about this N.E.O.Practice, please feel free to email me at victoria@1234neo.com*).

Habit No.5. Check documents, visas, and entry rules for the country you are going to three days before departure.

- Rules and laws often change. You will ensure a pleasant trip without delays at airports and borders.
- Get yourself a nice envelope or case for passports and travel documents.

Habit No.6. It is better to have cash with you.

- Take cash with you on the road and on small bills - don't forget to say thank you to yourself when it comes in handy. Your card or mobile phone payment may not work in different regions of the planet. Cash will protect you from thirst, hunger and bad mood.
- Gratitude tips are also better in cash.

Habit No.7. When leaving, leave a tidy room behind you.

- Order in your room, and order at home provides good energy and a clean N.E.O.Home.
- Thank the room before leaving. This is an energetically useful one-second thing.

Habit No.8. Encourage good service with tips.

- Gratitude can be expressed with a word, a look, or a tip. You give gratitude, and you receive the life energy of the Creator in return.

Habit No.9. Travel in two ways: both spontaneously and planned.

- Keep balance and enjoy in any case.
- Learn to use both methods - it will expand the neural network and increase the level of calmness in everyday life.

Habit No.10. Maintain your emotional balance.

- Attentiveness, vigilance, and calmness are the best companions in any journey. Take them with you!

9TH SPHERE. RHYTHM

Habit No.1. Review your priorities.

- We are constantly changing, and the world around us is also changing. What worked yesterday will not necessarily work tomorrow. Check your priorities for relevance.

- Build your priorities at the pace of a rapidly changing reality. Rearrange them, highlight the main and important ones, and align them with your life.

Habit No.2. Keep a balance between the comfort zone of the brain and the Flow of the Soul.

- This is the point of Well-Being: there are no imbalances toward rigid analysis or careless sloppiness.
- The brain wants to be in the comfort zone, and the soul wants to fly.

Habit No.3. Practice unhurriedness.

- Adjust your speed. "Haste makes waste."
- A calm inner state always brings the fruits of Well-Being.

Habit No.4. Don't put off until tomorrow what you can do today.

- Be vigilant about the rhythm of your movement.
- Procrastination is a sign of a lack of energy. If you notice it in yourself, immediately do an N.E.O.Pause for an inflow of energy.

Habit No.5. Translate life into your inner time.

- Horizontal time is called Chronos, and vertical time is called Kairos. And at their intersection is the present moment. Live in it.
- Living on inner time provides a resourceful state and a favorable series of events in your reality.

Habit No.6. Increase your awareness.

- The more pieces in your reality picture, the higher your awareness.
- Train attentiveness with N.E.O.Pauses.
- Holistic Well-Being is conditioned by high awareness.

Habit No.7. Practice calmness.

- Everything in this world is worthy of my calmness - tell yourself this in any stressful situation.
- When you are calm inside, this calmness spreads to people and situations.

Habit No.8. Keep a balance of work and rest.

- Work and rest by alternating.
- Introduce a musical rhythm into your life: DO-BE-DO-BE-DO: Do-Be-Do-Be-Do...
- The ability to rest is no less important than the ability to work.

Habit No.9. Keep moderation in everything.

- Don't try too hard. "Don't push the saw" - it slows down the process.
- Excessive effort and zeal cause an imbalance in moving toward the goal because tension arises in the energy field.
- Don't be lazy, don't be greedy, don't overexert yourself.

Habit No.10. Attune to the Flow.

- Everything happens appropriately and in a timely manner.
- To live in the Flow, do N.E.O.Pauses several times a day.

Practice the N.E.O.Affirmation: "Happiness fills my way, all works out day by day"

- Be aware in the moment of the universal cosmic rule: "It's not me. It's through me."

10TH SPHERE. MONEY

Habit No.1. Keep cash in order.

- Maintain order in your wallet.
- The wallet should appeal to you.

Habit No.2. Control your cash flows.

- Money loves to be counted - keep track of it in your head or write it down.
- Set a rule for yourself: Income exceeds expenses.

Habit No.3. Treat money with respect.

- Make it a habit for yourself, and you will see how the Money Flow will turn in your direction.
- Don't talk about money with sarcasm, and don't talk sarcastically about the lack of it; don't be ironic about your lack of money.
- Do you like jokes about money? And black humor on this topic? It's funny, but the Money Flow turns away from you.

Habit No.4. Manage the money flow.

- Create funds in your budget, as in a thriving corporation: for development, for investments, for travel, and to watch them grow.
- The energy of money is woven into the energy pattern of your N.E.O.Home.

Habit No.5. Learn to work with cash and non-cash money.

- Skillfully use payment cards, online payments, and bank accounts.
- Get to know your banker, and they will open up interesting opportunities for managing finances for you.
- Always have cash with you in a comfortable amount.

Habit No.6. Carefully provide financial assistance.

- Help where you can do it sincerely and without tension, the financial flows will turn to you.
- Money can help or harm. Check with your heart.

Habit No.7. Keep your intentions about money clean.

- The Money Flow is the energy that originates in your thoughts and intentions.
- Create businesses, projects, and strategies with pure intention, and the money flow will flow to you.

Habit No.8. Learn to invest.

- Invest with reason and without haste, without pressure from your loved ones, financial experts, or fashion trends. Hear the response inside yourself, and only then invest.

- Change the word "spend" in your vocabulary to "invest". Don't spend on yourself, everyday life, or pleasures, but invest in yourself, your life, and your pleasures.

Habit No.9. Trust and verify.

- Trust life, and check bills before signing.
- Money loves order. Order in money matters grows Well-Being.

Habit No.10. Live without debts.

- Living without debts is when you don't owe or are not owed.
- Respond carefully and thoughtfully to requests to borrow money. Money is energy that is introduced into relationships, even of the closest ones. If there is no response, don't lend money, and don't borrow.

CHAPTER 8.
VOLUNTARY EXIT
FROM THE COMFORT ZONE
IN A GIVEN DIRECTION

Our team has developed a Game with the help of which, you will easily and effortlessly be able to change your life through changing habits. Using the N.E.O.Workbook we offer, you can check which of the 100 described habits you already have, which of them you like, and which you would like to establish for yourself. Habits can be developed or used to replace old, outdated ones.

**CHANGING HABITS
IS POSSIBLE, EASY,
AND PLEASANT.**

To understand the algorithm for changing a habit, it is necessary to understand where its roots are. The mechanism of the habit itself is already a flower or a fruit that we taste daily in our lives. But this flower grows from the depths of our subconscious. And its source is at the point of our beliefs.

Beliefs are formed by trial and error. For example, you scalded yourself with boiling water as a child. You developed the belief that hot water is dangerous and painful. From this belief, from this feedback from reality, you build a picture of the world in which you will be very careful with hot water and everything related to it: a hot bath, a hot kettle, a hot cup, a pan, hot sand, and so on. The picture of the world, formed based on multiple beliefs growing from childhood, is actually your idea of this world. Therefore, the formation of the picture of the world is an extraordinarily important, vitally important process.

Example:

As a child, you had an experience where some big and strong boy, older than you, took away something dear to you: a candy or a toy. An inner conviction is formed in you, it depends on your system of perception with which you came to this Earth, into this incarnation. Based on this experience, completely different beliefs can arise. Someone will immediately think they want to be stronger than this strong one so no one else can take away what is dear. Another, due to their unique susceptibility, will come to the belief that everything needs to be hidden so that the stronger ones do not take it away. From these two different positions of perception of the world, a different system of values is formed.

The value system is the next level of the root system of a habit because principles are formed from the value system - the principles of general behavior and general perception of this world. Rules appear from principles. Rules can also be general or specific. A skill is already tied to the rules.

A habit is formed from a skill. Therefore, when we want to establish a habit, it is very important, first of all, to answer the questions for ourselves:

- What will this habit give you, and why do you need it?
- How will it make your life easier?
- What will it change?

These questions are not at all tricky and do not lead to abandoning a new habit; on the contrary, these questions help us to transfer the processes of developing a particular habit to the level of awareness with the motivation of necessity and importance. This helps to overcome laziness in developing habits and make the art of developing new habits an easy and pleasant game in everyday life.

HOW TO UNDERSTAND THE USEFULNESS OR HARMFULNESS OF CERTAIN HABITS FOR YOURSELF?

It is not necessary to reduce everything to black and white and to strictly classify each habit according to the concepts: good or bad, useful or harmful. But in order to understand the basis, it is enough to understand the energetic sign of a certain habit in your behavior model, in your character.

A useful (good) habit brings joy, satisfaction, a positive emotion, an inflow of energy, and a comforting, satisfactory final result. A harmful (bad) habit makes a person irritable, drooping, and upset, leads to dissatisfaction with the results obtained, and takes away vital energy.

So, the main criterion is the final result of the inner emotional state, worldview, level of joy, and state of affairs.

If, as a result of a certain habit, you get instant gratification, for example, from cigarettes, but in the long-term result, it leads to a weakening of health, then most likely such a habit needs to be replaced with a useful one.

It is very important to realize that there are no mistakes here - in this reality, so no matter what habits you discover in yourself, please do not be upset, but on the contrary, rejoice that you have realized that it is time to change this or that habit. Do not approach changing a habit as a marathon race - until I reach the finish line, I will not stop. Cancel old, outdated, and unnecessary habits with love for yourself. This will relieve stress from the process and shorten the time of refusal.

An example from my life of how I lost weight with the help of a bad habit:

Until age 40, I actively fought against excess weight, not realizing that the position of struggle never brings a long-term positive effect. Therefore, each new diet worked for a certain period, and due to life stresses of one magnitude or another or their accumulation, the diet ceased to be effective.

Once, I met my friend and was surprised at how significantly she had improved her figure and reduced the number of extra pounds. My friend recommended a nutritionist named Maria to me.

I came for an appointment, not knowing that Maria's first education was a brilliant clinical psychiatrist with many years of experience in European clinics.

Maria asked me about my lifestyle, diet, and eating habits. Listening to me as a professional psychiatrist, she realized the extent of my stress accumulated over the years and asked me a simple question: "If you could eat absolutely everything, at any time of the day or night, without restrictions, how would you eat?"

I thought deeply and was rather at a dead end, and I had never imagined such a state in which I was not limited by anything. Then, having gathered all the boldest ideas about life, I told Maria, "I would have a cappuccino with whole milk and cake every day at five o'clock in the evening."

To my great surprise, Maria said: "Great. That's where we'll start." This was an unexpected turn of events, and I began to follow the nutritionist's recommendations.

Every day I ate cake and cappuccino at five o'clock, and from all my points of view, this was a very bad habit. But phenomenally, my weight began to go down, contrary to any laws of nutrition, calorie counting, and reasonableness.

Of course, I established this habit for myself for only a few months, very quickly realizing that I was ready to reduce the calorie content and size of the cake, replace whole milk with low-fat milk in my cappuccino, take care of the flour from which this cake was baked, and during these few months, I brought my habit of traditional coffee at five o'clock to a light snack.

This example taught me that any habit, even the most harmful one, can be useful for a short period if it provides the unloading of our emotional and nervous systems. Remember this when you consciously eliminate or replace an unnecessary habit in your character. Act with love, a smile, and awareness.

HABIT AS AN ASSISTANT IN NEUTRALIZING STRESS AND TENSION

The example described above is also about the anti-stress effect of some habits. Let it be temporary, but definitely working.

Of the 100 Well-Being habits described in this book, several specifically neutralize stress and tension. The development of such habits provides a more stable mental and emotional state. Any useful habit is an assistant in the harmonious flow of life. But some habits are directly capable of turning stress into a source of good mood in the moment. (*See the catalog of habits in Chapter 7, spheres: Mood, Thoughts, Body*)

DISCIPLINE IS DIFFERENT: VOLITIONAL AND NATURAL

Speaking about developing new habits, it is impossible not to talk about discipline. But we will look at discipline from a slightly different angle.

There are a huge number of books on how discipline is important and necessary in developing habits. But it is very important to understand that discipline can have different states.

Discipline can be volitional, or it can be natural.

In order to develop a habit, we need willpower - **volitional discipline.** The duration of such volitional discipline (provided that the process itself is conscious and understanding why this or that habit is needed[2]) is a certain number of days. [2]According to scientists - some say it is 21 days. In some studies of one of the English colleges - it is 66 days. But at the same time, the figure was different for everyone - from 18 to 254 days. We are all unique. This must be remembered. Therefore, volitional discipline, when we hold the focus of attention, works with resistance that arises constantly and by force will go to the daily result, rhythmically and constantly - this volitional discipline is needed only until the habit is established.

---

[2] We suggest you try the exercise described in the Workbook – this will help you understand the importance of establishing certain habits specifically for yourself.

But then the habit becomes our assistant in the discipline. When a habit is developed, for example, making the bed, this habit becomes **a natural discipline**, which means that now we do it automatically, thereby organizing our energy space thoughts in our head and ensuring a sufficient amount of vital energy for life in the flow. Everyone has discipline. To one degree or another, we all possess this wonderful quality.

The basis of discipline is habits, and discipline is needed to develop a habit. Let's not categorically divide habits into difficult and easy to develop. It's individual. It is very easy for someone to wake up to an alarm clock at 6 am and do exercises, while for someone else, it is very hard work. Therefore, everyone determines which habit is easy and which is difficult to develop.

Remember, volitional discipline is only needed for a couple of weeks, and then the habit itself builds a prosperous life for you in a natural disciplinary order.

HELPFUL TIPS FOR NEW HABITS

1. Realize what habit you want to develop and answer the questions for yourself: What will this habit give me, and why do I need it? How will it make my life easier, and what will this habit change in my life?
2. Don't overdo it with discipline. Don't put pressure on yourself - it's like pushing on a saw. It only slows down the sawing

process. Don't forget that life should be like beautiful music, alternating beats: DO-BE-DO-BE-DO...
3. Develop new habits with ease and pleasure.
4. Patience and a playful approach are helpers in developing new habits.
5. Develop habits gradually. Our N.E.O.Workbook helps you connect imaginative thinking, good mood and a game method to habit formation.

WHAT IS MORE IMPORTANT IN DEVELOPING A HABIT – MEANING OR METHODOLOGY?

I think that both meaning and methodology or rather, the way to develop a habit into your character and routine, are equally important values. At the same time, for each of us, unique in our energetic, mental, biological, physiological, and all other structures, it is important to realize what is specifically important for you and act in proportion to your feelings and convictions.

So, meaning lies at the core. Meaningless habit formation or meaningless habits is of no interest to anyone. But even if we see meaning, but at the same time do not determine for ourselves in what way we can move in the direction of this meaning, then most likely, the meaning will move away from us or remain at the same distance, like a carrot on a string in front of a donkey's nose.

To determine the meaning of developing a habit, do the exercise in our N.E.O.Workbook that comes with this book. If the answers to the test questions are positive for you and you feel a surge of strength and good mood from passing the meaning test for developing a habit, then this habit is definitely necessary and will be useful for you. Feel the system intuitively. Listen to yourself, listen with your heart, trust yourself.

TAKING INVENTORY OF YOUR HABITS IS A USEFUL THING.

Before developing new habits or getting rid of old ones, it is very important to realize the existing ones and their impact on your life.

In our N.E.O.Workbook for this book, there is a special section that helps to take inventory of your habits, prioritize them, and answer the question for yourself: Do I still need this habit, or should I replace it with a new one?

At the same time, a real approach is important, without illusions.

Based on research by scientists that we perform 90% of our life's habitual, automatic actions, the realization naturally emerges that many of our habits are unknown to us; we do not notice them. Perhaps we have had them since childhood, simply copied from the manners and behaviors of our parents, grandparents, relatives, and friends, the group in kindergarten and school. Therefore, when doing such an inventory, I recommend doing it not on the run but thoughtfully, sensibly, and with arrangement.

The more of the existing habits we are able to realize, the faster the road to Well-Being and the clearer and more specific the improvement in the quality of life. You can sit down and think about this task. You can think about it by observing your behavior during the week. I recommend that you combine these two methods and start the self-study of your habits by sitting down with the N.E.O.Workbook, pondering, answering the test questions, and then, during the week, noticing and writing down all the habits that you notice more and at the end of the week finalizing in a special section of the N.E.O.Workbook a list of your habits, dividing them into two categories: "I need it" and "I don't need it." After that, it will be easier for you to choose new habits to develop into your rhythm of life and character.

FREQUENCY AND PURITY OF HABITS

Different habits have different frequencies.

For example, the habit of brushing your teeth - for some, it is once a day. For others, it is twice a day, and for some, brushing their teeth after every meal is a habit. The habit of morning exercises can only be once a day or three times a week, but it cannot be several times a day.

There are habits, the frequency of which, for example, is once a year - the habit of gathering the whole family at the dinner table for Christmas or a birthday. When I was a child, I had the habit of trying seasonal watermelon for the first time on my birthday on July 17. Of course, such a habit ceased to be relevant, but it stayed in my life for a long time and brought me joy.

Some habits are repeated once a week, for example, the habit of quality cleaning in the house. Usually, a certain day of the week is set aside for such a habit, which is associated with many other smaller habits that make cleaning the house a joyful and meaningful event.

When developing a new habit, don't forget to note for yourself what frequency it has. It is very difficult to develop several daily habits at the same time. But to decide for yourself that this month I will develop five new habits, of which one will be daily, two will be weekly, one will be monthly, and another will be annual - this is not difficult at all. This way, you can develop several habits in one month without tension and with pleasure.

At the same time, the purity of your habit always depends on pure intention and an open heart. If developing a habit is a pleasant and joyful event for you, then the purity of the habit will be high, which means it will always bring a lot of positive life energy into your life.

WHAT HELPS IN DEVELOPING A NEW HABIT?

Statistics say that more than 50% of people who try to develop a new habit give up this idea after a maximum of six months. In my opinion, the reason for this is insufficient motivation. And what can be the best motivation for our N.E.O.Home? This is undoubtedly a state of pleasure, satisfaction, and, as a result, joy in the soul from any action. Therefore, if you need to develop a useful habit that is difficult for you to develop, then come up with a positive game action or a small ritual associated with this habit.

For example, you want to teach yourself not to scatter things but to put them in their places immediately, but because you haven't done this for many years in a row, and now there is an urgent need (for example, you started living with a partner who does not tolerate scattered things, and you, taking care of your relationship, decided to develop this new habit for yourself) - make a bonus ritual for yourself: whenever you put your things in place, go to the mirror and say to yourself: "I love you!"

Such a motivating mini-ritual will have a double positive effect and maybe even a triple one. You will always smile at this and at yourself in the mirror, you will fold things with pleasure, and you will also miraculously fill yourself with life energy at the moment from this simple affirmation.

Developing habits is also helped by the support of like-minded people, which is why there are now so many different communities in which people unite in small interest groups.

The next helping factor may be the support of your household members, so don't be afraid to share your intention to develop new useful habits with the people you live under the same roof with, and then you will have a support group. If you know that one of your household members may make barbs or black humor towards you, you do not need to share your initiative with them. Make sure that the process of developing a new habit is stress-free for you.

Another very good motivating ritual for useful household habits is music. Turn on the music you love and combine the new habit with a certain playlist. You can even create a special playlist for a specific habit. This will also be a motivation for you.

WHAT TO DO IF THERE IS RESISTANCE TO A NEW HABIT?

Resistance will arise in almost 95% of cases of developing a new habit, and this can happen at different phases. Sometimes resistance turns on immediately; sometimes, as statistics say, it can catch up with you after six months.

When developing a habit, it is very important to understand why it is needed, what we expect from its development, and what changes it will bring. Our N.E.O.Workbook will help you.

The very nature of the brain function provides resistance. The brain loves the comfort zone - stable, limited, clear states without changes and innovations; therefore, on the one hand, an established habit is a support for the brain, and on the other hand, the brain terribly does not like to change anything, i.e., to leave the comfort zone. The brain's resistance can be expressed in different forms and in different ways, from sabotage to melancholy. Smile at this, realizing the attempts of your brain to turn on the blocking of changes for the better in your life.

There is one more point: you may have incorrectly determined the meaning of the habit for yourself, you begin to develop it, and you feel that it significantly irritates you and does not make you happy. Then take the "100 Habits" N.E.O.Workbook in your hands once again and once again think about whether the goals and meanings of developing this habit are relevant, or you did not quite correctly assess the need for such a habit.

The most important thing is that developing a habit is a creative living process.

Do not try to fit it into some standard template or someone else's experience. I would even say that developing a new habit is a creative process without rules, but there are states, feelings, desires, and joy. Then, the resistance of the brain is not scary either.

HOW MANY HABITS DOES A PERSON NEED FOR A PROSPEROUS LIFE?

Immanuel Kant said: "The more habits, the less freedom." But at the same time, without a doubt, Kant had in mind that, on average, we act automatically 90% of the time in everyday life. Therefore, the ratio of 90 to 10 is actually living in an unconscious state. By bringing habits to the level of awareness, conducting an inventory, and cleaning periodically in our lives, we achieve the freedom Kant spoke about.

Several habits are necessary for us. Being 100% conscious is very energy-consuming, so we must realize that there should be just enough habits to create the basis for our Well-Being and not limit our free creative life in the flow. Balance, as you know, is the optimal solution.

This is the middle path that Buddhism speaks of.

No one can tell us how many habits each person needs, but everyone can feel it in their heart and choose useful good habits for themselves, develop them into their character, and live prosperously.

CHAPTER 9.
DAILY WELL-BEING RITUALS

Here, I want to share with you my daily Well-Being practices.

We will talk about daily rituals - reading, Well-Being habits - as ways to maintain a resourceful state or a state of Well-Being throughout the day, the whole week, the whole life.

I really devote a lot of time during the day to maintaining a resourceful state, and I did not learn this right away, but over time, the skill came, and it became a habit, so now it does not take a lot of attention and amount of life energy to organize this process, everything happens by itself.

YOU NEED TO TAKE CARE OF YOUR WELL-BEING

What is important in the topic of daily rituals?

In this topic, it is important to realize a simple truth: to be truly prosperous - and this means to be healthy financially, in relationships, and in self-realization - you need to take care of this Well-Being. This is not an automatic process at all. I have devoted a lot of time in my life to studying jurisprudence in different countries, and I can tell you there is such a phenomenon that people sometimes do not realize.

Some people think that in jurisprudence, everything happens automatically since there is a law for it. In fact, nothing happens automatically. If you want to get something according to the law, you must file a petition for everything. The same is true in universal law - cosmic law. If you want to get Well-Being for yourself, take care of it. Take care of it with the help of various Practices that you will implement into your life, just as I gradually introduced them over the past 30 years, and this will ultimately bring a positive result.

Good news: you don't need 30 years to search for practices. I have gathered them in this book and will share them with you. You will be able to integrate them into your rhythm of life in a convenient way. A prerequisite: each practice each technique must be repeated systematically. A practice that we have written down somewhere and forgotten, a practice that we once listened to and learned about, a practice that we have done three times - none of this works. It is necessary to practice the practice.

THE MORE WE THANK, THE MORE LIFE ENERGY COMES TO US

To benefit means to Bene-give and Bene-thank. This is a universal formula. The more we invest in our Well-Being, the more Well-Being we have.

Please relax. Now is N.E.O.Pause

This is the simplest technique of a resourceful state that I use during the day. I use different N.E.O.Pauses, but I consider the key one to be

the N.E.O.Pause of Well-Being,

which is essentially

the Practice of Gratitude.

First, we bene-give, and after that comes the process of bene-receiving.

Read the description of the practice

and do it right away.

It will take 3 minutes.

We take a comfortable position. If we are sitting or standing, straighten the shoulders. If we are lying down, straighten the back. It is important that the channel is open at all levels, in all bodies: both in the physical body and in our mental body - we will tune our thoughts to gratitude, and in our vital body - we will emotionally return to ourselves, concentrate and be only in the present moment, so all our bodies must be ready. For this, it is physically enough to straighten the back, throw off the burden of tension from the shoulders, smile, and close the eyes. Inhale and exhale.

This is the N.E.O.Pause of Gratitude; it transfers us to the present moment, and we maintain the focus of our attention in the present moment by observing the breath. We observe our breath without hurrying, without straining, without interfering with it. Just observe. Observing the breath calms the emotions and synchronizes our vibrations with the vibration of the present moment.

We immerse deeper into ourselves by transferring attention to the center of the head, behind the eyes. In the center of the head, we feel our presence and transfer it to the collarbones, shoulders, elbows, and palms. In the palms, we feel ourselves - this can manifest as a sensation of warmth, tingling, and coolness. Everything is fine and not necessary.

We transfer attention to the navel.

Again, we observe the breath. We move attention to the knees, relax them, and completely relax the legs. Let's shift attention to the feet and realize what they touch: insoles, slippers, carpet, floor, snow, grass... Let's focus on the center of the chest, the heart. We allow ourselves to shine. Light comes out of the heart and flows in streams throughout the body. This is the light of love. The heart is a channel through which light, passing through us, illuminates the whole body and the space around us. An open heart is the basis of Well-Being. Let's realize that this is a gift - the ability to shine in the dark, that each of us is a star that knows how to shine, and it needs nothing for this. We are grateful for this gift. We thank the Higher Forces, we thank Mother Earth, we thank the Sun and the Moon. We thank Life - a living entity. We thank ourselves for doing this N.E.O.Pause and thereby filling ourselves with life energy.

We thank. We will smile and open our eyes.

PRACTICES OF A RESOURCEFUL STATE

What is important to understand initially: the rituals of consciously directing attention to the present moment, which I call daily rituals of Well-Being, are important because we work with our attention.

In order to maintain our resourceful state, we don't need anything. When transferring attention to the present moment, it is enough to feel yourself here and now - it is at this moment we connect to the resource and are filled.

The brain's task is to lead us away from here because the brain loves to live in the future or in the past. The saturation with life energy occurs in the present moment, so the meaning of all daily rituals of Well-Being comes down to the same thing: it is returning yourself to the present moment.

My rituals are enhanced by the fact that I add some practices to them, and because I have always been a busy and active person, in fact, I do a long meditation as the main practice of filling myself with life energy only twice a day: 20-30 minutes in the morning and 10-15 minutes in the evening. I can't do more because I want to have time to do a lot of other things.

Note that I'm not saying I don't have time for this. No, time has nothing to do with it. The key here is life energy. In order to organize your day, you must have a sufficient amount of life energy. Since the organization takes time, I understand this and calculate my life energy practically during the day.

I have some rituals on hand that I turn on when I feel a drop in energy, and I have some arsenal for different occasions, which is always at hand, and I can turn it on.

I try to replenish my resources rhythmically during the day and not wait for the state when the energy has already dropped and I need to do something about it. That is, I am constantly recharging and investing time in myself in advance, so that the resourceful state is constantly high.

I have mandatory morning rituals, evening rituals, and rituals that I use throughout the day.

MORNING RITUALS FOR A PROSPEROUS DAY

The moment I wake up, when I just touch reality with my attention, at that very moment I immediately direct my attention to a prosperous reality. I will greet this day inside myself, I will smile at the sun, and thank this day for being so wonderful. And I call this practice "Awakening into a prosperous reality."

The first practice every morning is waking up to a prosperous reality. It is enough to be in this state for one minute. After that, I can allow myself to think about something calmly, but it depends on whether I have a free minute or a reason to hurry. If I understand that

I have limited time, I immediately practice getting up correctly. The correct getting up takes me about a minute and a half. In fact, it is a short warm-up and stretching while lying down. (*Many examples can be found freely available on YouTube*).

Before brushing my teeth, I comb my hair and "align" my thoughts. A combed head, like a made bed, is actually very important. This is what creates a prosperous environment inside our field - an emotional calm. When combing my hair in front of the mirror, I always smile at myself sometimes, I can say: "I love you!" (*this is Louise Hay's technique*).

After the mandatory hygienic procedures, I go out to the kitchen - where I have my own rituals and the first ritual is that I drink warm purified water, talking to it. I thank the water for charging me for the whole day.

At the same time as drinking water, I apply essential oil to my wrists and palms (I always have several different scents at hand; I choose by feeling which one is needed right now) and inhale several times.

Next, I definitely do the oiling procedure - I Swallow a mixture of a tablespoon of vegetable oil with citrus juice. I use natural first, cold-pressed olive oil. I mix the oil one-on-one with lemon juice or something citrus juice- bergamot, grapefruit, or lime. And before I oil myself, I definitely talk to this oil.

At the moment of mixing the oil with citrus juice, I talk into this oil everything that I want to wish for myself for this day - on some days, I want to wish myself vigor. On some days, lightness; on some days, luck, but on any day, I want to wish myself a lot of love in my life and excellent health, and these are not memorized phrases. This is not a mantra that is read, this is a live conversation with the product that I will take inside.

My next morning ritual is that I take spirulina, which helps me alkalize my body. Of course, the best way to alkalize the body is to hold the breath, but I have rather short breath holds, so I help myself with spirulina. When choosing spirulina, I always pay attention to the manufacturer and the quality of the product.

After the "kitchen rituals," I go to do practices - on average, it takes me one hour. Sometimes, I try to do it faster; I experiment a lot, but there is a base that is unchanged.

What are practices?

These are four parts:

- Warm-up
- Breathing practices
- Energy practices
- Meditation

I have collected my warm-up gradually over many years. I have been doing the warm-up for about 25 years, almost every day, very rarely when I violate this ritual of mine. I warm up all body parts

- from the crown to the feet. From time to time, I change my complex because the brain begins to get used to it, and at some point, I catch myself moving my arms/legs, and my brain is already somewhere in the future or in the past. It is necessary to periodically refresh the training elements to prevent this from happening.

To date, my warm-up includes a set of exercises for the whole body: for all joints, for strengthening the spine, for correct posture - all this together takes me 20 minutes.

Then, I do separate exercises for harmonizing the hemispheres - this takes another 7-10 minutes.

Then I have breathing practices - it also takes about 10 minutes, then I move on to energy practices.

Energy practices are special exercises, together with visualization, which help to fully restore our field structure - the Torus - to be in a harmonious state so that the energies flow well, and I devote another 10 minutes to this.

After that, I go into meditation for 30 minutes.

This is what I do every morning. And it takes a maximum of an hour and a half. But it's worth it to charge up for the whole day and spend it as efficiently as possible. I recommend ending the morning rituals with a green smoothie.

Then, during the day, I do various micro-practices, N.E.O.Pauses.

Please relax. Now is N.E.O.Pause

And now the N.E.O.Pause –

Harmonization of the hemispheres

Read the description of the practice

and do it right away.

It will take 1 minute.

The exercise is called "Criss Cross": With the right hand, we take the lobe of the left ear, with the left hand - the tip of the nose. Hands cross. Then, with the left hand we will take the right ear, and with the right hand - the nose. So, we alternately change the position of the hands. We start slowly, and if possible, we accelerate.

At the same time, you need to make sure, firstly, that there is a smile on your face (if we load too much, then it is better to slow down), and secondly, we focus on the fact that your hands actually touch a certain place - the earlobe and the tip of the nose. Such a very clear hit at the very point can be a goal and really helps harmonize the hemispheres. Practice every day.

Continuing on the morning rituals, it is very important to note that I do not pick up the phone for the first 10 minutes after waking up. I don't look at any messages. I don't check social networks. The discipline not to allow me to hang on the mobile phone required some effort on my part, but ultimately led me to a completely wonderful state of absolute freedom from the mobile phone. It is always with me, but I only take it into my hands when there is a work necessity.

Another important Well-Being ritual is to necessarily pour water over yourself or take a shower or bath twice a day. Water is a universal conductor and purifier; that is, by cleansing with water, we cleanse our physical body and all our subtle bodies.

EVENING RITUALS FOR GOOD SLEEP AND A PROSPEROUS TOMORROW

In addition to water procedures, a cleansing meditation is a must in the evening. This meditation takes 10-15 minutes, usually, I do it every evening before going to bed.

I breathe White Light and tell myself that it cleanses me. This is a meditation that happens in silence - I just observe my breathing, how the white light enters me and exits, cleansing my body. After that I go to bed and do the N.E.O.Pause for fast falling asleep.

For fast falling asleep, it is easiest to observe your breathing. As soon as I start observing the breath, everything calms down, and sleep comes by itself. Such a pure technique - conscious falling asleep - is especially suitable for those who practice lucid dreaming.

What else is important is that you should not fall asleep with a mobile phone in your hands; this is an indispensable condition for harmonious falling asleep, after which it is very easy to sleep all night, and it is easy to wake up in the morning.

MICRO RITUALS - N.E.O.PAUSES FOR MAINTAINING A PROSPEROUS DAY

There are other techniques that I use daily throughout the day.

Gratitude for food

First of all, it is **the ritual of Gratitude for food**. Any food, before eating it, I thank it. If I eat or snack alone, then I do it mentally. But if I am having breakfast, lunch, or dinner with someone, then we hold hands and thank out loud.

You can call it a prayer before meals. I call it the N.E.O.Pause of Gratitude for food, which always begins with the words: "Thank you, Creator..." "Creator" here is more of an appeal to what is familiar to our brain, but of course, everyone can call in their way that great Force that gives us this life, which actually creates this life, and no matter what we call it, it is very right to thank it for the meal. To thank the people who contributed to this delicious food being on our table and the guests for being with us at this meal - all this together creates the N.E.O.Pause of Gratitude before eating. This is a mandatory Well-Being ritual that is present in my daily schedule.

Supporting affirmations

What else do I use during the day - these are **different affirmations**. I sing them. I have such affirmations that I create myself in poetic form for different occasions.

For example, there are affirmations for lifting the mood: "I am cheerful and merry. My affairs are good." I will repeat such an affirmation three times out loud. I can sing it, chant it - and immediately, the vibration changes, and this is felt at the level of all bodies.

And when I feel that the inflow of funds and material Well-Being suddenly worries me (Attention! This has nothing at all to do with the funds or material Well-Being themselves; it's just that sometimes the brain gives us such anxiety signals), I remove these signals with the affirmation: " Wealth and success light my way, bringing fortune day by day." In exactly the same way, I will definitely say it three times: I can sing it.

If I feel that, for example, the topic of health worries me, then I use the N.E.O.Pause with the affirmation: "Health and beauty, grace divine, make my life so brightly shine."

All these affirmations I once created for myself, wrote them down, learned them - they come at the request. If you, having tuned in, sit down and ask life for an affirmation, it will come down to you - exactly the one that suits you.

In case when I am tired when I understand that I feel fatigued and I don't have the opportunity to rest now, I use a very working affirmation that I came up with when I worked on the project "I can do": "With 'can do,' I play all day, finding rest along the way." - I tell myself this three times, and it really works.

The point is that when we pronounce affirmations, we are in the present moment; we are not distracted by anything, and these few seconds during which we immerse ourselves in the present moment with the help of affirmation are the most valuable. It is they who return energy to us at all levels.

JOY IS THE STATE OF THE NEW TIME

Throughout the day, I use **the N.E.O.Pause of Joy** many times - this is when I close my eyes, transfer my attention inside myself, see the light, and say: "Joy fills me." At this moment, I understand that the light that fills me brings me joy, and I consciously live in this state here and now.

A very good **ritual is a Smile**. As soon as we smile, we immediately transmit it to the space, to the reality around us - and the space responds with a corresponding vibration. A smile is an amazing Well-Being ritual. It always works. You don't need to invent anything for this. Just smile. Smile at yourself in the mirror, smile at people, smile at trees and birds. Smile from the heart - and this will create a smile in the soul, a smile on the face.

This returns joy.

Joy is the point from which one needs to live in this millennium, so the rituals of Well-Being associated with returning joy to yourself several times a day are as mandatory as washing your hands. This is even a much more effective remedy against viral (and non-viral) infections than washing your hands. As soon as we return to joy, we raise our vibration, and there, viruses have no chance of attaching to us at those frequencies.

THE PRACTICE OF ADMIRATION

The next practice of daily rituals is **the practice of Admiration**. It is the habit of admiring - from the word lubo to love - to admire something. As a rule, we know how to admire our children, we know how to admire a loved one, we sometimes know how to admire ourselves if we like ourselves in the mirror, we admire something that is beautiful to us. In the same way, you can learn to admire what seems ordinary to us. Just look at it with different eyes - the eyes of those in love, eyes that transfer this love from our heart to the subject we are looking at.

There is another ritual, it is used when I want to admire, but I can't admire something or someone. This **ritual is called: "Three**

Beauties": in everything that I don't like, that causes irritation or discontent, I immediately look for three beauties in it.

Often in our lives, in communication with people, situations occur when we can't even perceive something, let alone admire it because we are out of sorts. After all, we admire from a state of sufficiency. Admiration is seeing with the eyes of the heart, that is, seeing from a resourceful state. And when we are upset, preoccupied or embittered - we can't admire, we have no resource to admire. Then a practice comes to the rescue - first, we find three beauties: in a Person, in a situation, in the current moment/space, and then we admire. It always works and always helps.

RAISING VIBRATIONS WITH SOUND

What else raises vibrations? It is **listening to mantras, classical music, high-vibrational texts from enlightened masters, and reading spiritual literature**.

Listening can be combined with walking - one of my daily rituals is to walk 10,000 steps - this raises the energy level even more.

HOW TO MAINTAIN A RESOURCEFUL STATE THROUGHOUT THE DAY

In conclusion, I want to convey a very important thing to you. I will convey it through a metaphor.

Imagine riding a bicycle in the summer on a flat path, surrounded by beauty, and everything is fine. Such a bicycle ride can be compared to living in a resource - a prosperous life.

Suddenly, an ascent begins. In order for you to maintain your pace, what do you need to do? It is imperative to start making more effort.

The same thing happens to us during the day.

We wake up in the morning - we are cheerful, have a lot of strength, start moving, and then situations, circumstances come, and events that take away our energy, which is normal. To maintain the pace, we need to pedal more intensively and to replenish this energy consumption for the whole day, we use daily practices - Well-Being rituals.

By doing so, we maintain a resourceful state throughout the day until late evening, and we even have the strength to do an evening meditation.

After all, you need strength to sit down to meditate in the evening after an intense day. Because when there is no strength, the brain will find a thousand reasons why you can skip meditation today.

More than once, I was led by what my brain tells me, and I understand how it works afterward, how it affects falling asleep, the next morning, the next week, and how all this ultimately affects the Well-Being of my life.

Please relax. Now is N.E.O.Pause

And I have one more N.E.O.Pause for you for 60 seconds - **N.E.O.Pause of Silence.**

Read the description of the practice and do it right away.

We will close our eyes, straighten our backs, straighten our shoulders, smile, and do nothing. Just stay in silence for a minute. Take a deeper breath and exhale, smile, and open your eyes.

I recommend doing N.E.O.Pauses daily throughout the day because by doing so, we unite energy into the common network of Light of our planet, and this is very important. The more we shine, the more light there is around.

You don't need to dispel the darkness; it's enough to radiate light.

CONCLUSION AND WISHES

To fit all Well-Being into 100 habits is, of course, impossible. And you may ask me a fair question: "Why is nothing said about sugar in the "Food" section? Can it be consumed without restrictions?" No, it is not necessary. Sugar is indeed harmful in excessive amounts for our protein body. But this book doesn't mention this eating habit. And so it is in many areas. There are only ten habits in each that I feel are relevant right now and in the lightness, without the hassle, in which the current life energies call us to live and act.

Will there be another book? With other Well-Being habits? I don't know yet. But I do know that each of you has habits that you want to share with other people.

Please write to me about what other habits were not included in this book but, based on your experience, lead to Well-Being, health, kind relationships, material prosperity, and self-realization.

Contact Me

You can reach me via email at victoria@1234neo.com or connect with me on social media at victoria_contoret.

Your feedback will be valuable not only for me but also for all N.E.O.People. I will come up with a way to share your feedback with N.E.O.People around the world.

Leave Your Feedback Here

When we sincerely share our experiences, joy, and good mood, the world becomes brighter and more prosperous.

Live Prosperously!

GRATITUDE

I am grateful to Life and the Creator for the people, circumstances, and opportunities I have encountered on my life's journey, where I realized that my Well-Being is my choice.

I thank my grandchildren, Shanti and Samuel because it is to them that I wanted and want to pass on the 100 Habits of Well-Being, and it seemed to me that this would be the best way: to write a book for everyone that my grandchildren will read.

Thank you to my daughter, Alexandra. She has been my guiding star for all 35 years of searching for and finding my Well-Being.

I thank each reader for their invaluable gift of attention to this book.

Produced by:

Editor: Tatyana Vakhnyuk
Proofreader: David Ibikunle
Cover Design: Tatyana Vakhnyuk

Font Credits:

Acme – SIL Open Font License, Copyright © 2011, Juan Pablo del Peral (juan@huertatipografica.com.ar), with Reserved Font Names "Acme"

Lemon Tuesday Regular 400 – SIL Open Font License, Copyright © 2016, Daria Kwon & Jovanny Lemonad

Made in the USA
Las Vegas, NV
24 February 2025